S

to

Soul Full

by
June Moore

A Soulfull
of Love June
x

Published in 2015 by SotH Publishing

ISBN
Paperback: 978-0-9931757-1-8
eBook: 978-0-9931757-0-1

A CIF Catalogue copy of this book is available from
the British Library

Published with the help of Indie Authors World

Dedication

This book is dedicated to the 'Kate's' in my life... My Nany Kate who was my beautiful soul mentor, my daughter Siobhan Kate who is my world, and my niece Amy Kate, the first of all my little ones, who, together with all my grandchildren, remind me to lighten up!

Preface

I am not a famous celebrity; neither am I so 'fool' of myself that I think my life journey is any more important than yours. I truly believe we all matter in the grand scheme of life. All our soul stories and experiences, no matter how they appear to others, impact not only upon our soul's growth but also on those who share our journeys, and on the world around us.

My story may be an ordinary one, filled with family problems, relationship issues, money issues, the normal 'stuff' we all have in common, and yet each unique soul can relate to it in their own way because it is the journey from head to heart, the most important journey we will ever make in our lifetime. This book is about the varied challenges and experiences from childhood, whether self-imposed or learned from our parents and others who impact upon our lives. It is about the patterns, programmes, habits, addictions, and limiting beliefs we hold or download from our forefathers and mothers, all of what we experience from birth.

When we arrive on this planet as a beautiful egoless, loving, hopeful soul in our little physical body, we are not aware of what life trials and tribulations our journey may have in store for us. From then on, many things can happen around us and yet we may never realise just how much those experiences may have impacted upon us. Some souls travel through emotional wars, mental wars or global wars. Some souls experience physical challenges, mental or emotional challenges, even material challenges. We are all brave, strong, wise, and ancient beings that choose to live life on this Earth, and yet, while our expansive and wise soul is incarnated in our body, it is the tricks of our mind which can work for or against us, that feed us fear, limiting beliefs, and create chaos. This imbalance between our heart and our mind is the reason many of us go round that revolving hamster wheel of dramas, problems, and patterns, stopping us from becoming the best version of ourselves that we came here to be.

My own life has been a series of dramas, 'mistakes', problems, fears and issues. Like many others, I had never taken time to look at it, always too busy inside my head or outside of myself, rescuing others, more focused on their lives rather than my own. But sometimes a higher force will find a way to stop that hamster wheel and bring you to your senses.

When life had led me to the bottomless pit of no money, no relationship, no business, and no hope – I ended up plastered!

Now alcohol had featured heavily in my life but in this case, I actually fell over my vacuum cleaner and broke my foot. This imposed time out made me truly turn inwards. Where was I heading? What was I doing? I was 57 and I knew my soul had a plan for me, but I had constantly been too busy thinking about everyone else's life to invest in my own, to partake in my own soul mission, to truly look at my soul map.

It was time to begin a new journey, one of the heart instead of the head, one of alchemy and transformation. I hope my life, my journey, can spark a new path for you, whatever your age. One where your mind is not solely in control but in perfect balance with your heart. A chance for your soul to take you on an immense journey without fears crippling you, without family patterns becoming your limiting patterns, without programmes that your mind adopted from your parents. Instead of allowing all these to keep you on that hamster wheel of recurring issues in your life, it's time to break free and live the life you came to explore.

My journey is now the basis of my work, which is called Science of the Heart. It is my soul work, my soul mission, and I am now grateful for all the experiences of my past. In seeing the gold within them all, I can look at life now through my soul's eyes and not the thoughts of my mind. I am free now to be all I wish to be, to be the best version of me as a soul with a body – no labels, no judgements attached that refer to me as a wife, mum, nana, businesswoman, or even as one of life's victims who lost it all.

I love my journey, and I love helping others to enjoy and appreciate their own journeys more now. I watch them becoming stronger from the path they have walked, gaining strength, wisdom, and insight into the path of their infinite dreams, whatever they may be.

I realised after I began this written journey that it had morphed from being called either 'Diary of Drama Queen' or 'Memoirs of a Mad Housewife' into something very different. I dropped much of the drama that peppered most of my life, stopped feeding the energy of pain and emotional trauma, looked at all the stories and saw the amazing gift which it had all been.

I let go of anger, frustration, and despair, and found the gold within. And I was guided to start this story again, from a different angle, from the beginning of my life, highlighting how I took on many programmes of rejection, parental patterns, and issues. I had rambled through life, adopted 'stuff' from other people who shared my life. This visit back in time to relive the soul map of my life was the most healing gift I have ever given myself. I saw the gold in the journey and I realised that alchemy was indeed happening. I let go of the lead weights and the baggage, and felt the freedom from fear and worry; a glorious golden gift.

I urge you, fellow soul traveller, to map out your own life, see the patterns you wish to change, the fears that hold you back, the programmes you are unaware of from childhood, and to transform your precious journey for the golden soul you already are!

Enjoy a golden life, whatever you choose.

About this book

I have included some soul conversations with myself into the text - like light bulb moments. They are called **Soul Notes** and are italicised for ease of reading. Write your own soul notes as you journey back through time and create the soul map of your life.

At the end of each chapter, each decade of my life, there will be at 'look back' or look at the back, a reference to how the journey of alchemy began. But I will leave it up to you, dear traveller, whether you leave the alchemy of the story to the end – as I did – or begin seeing the alchemy in each stage of your life.

At the end of the book, you will find a short guide to the seven stages of alchemy relating to the journey I have undergone on my way from head to heart.

I truly hope your soul map is amazing, healing, inspiring and insightful. Enjoy an inner journey to find a more peaceful, limitless you, a journey of freedom from your head to your golden empowered heart.

Chapter 1

1950s – The journey begins

It was on 10th June, 1952, at exactly 10pm that I entered my new world! A beautiful little baby girl, whose proud parents, John and Elsie, could not envisage naming me anything other than the month I was born in!

(Soul note: lack of imagination alert in this family!)

Having made quite an impact on them with my loud, nonstop screeching, I was placed into the loving arms of one beautiful soul – Kate Wilson, my eternally loving Nany. No, not a nanny, just in case you thought my beginnings were of great wealth and grandeur, but my grandmother – Catharine Clements Geddes Wilson, my ever-teaching, ever-loving, soul mentor. Little did I know in those early days how much of an impact she would have on my future life.

I don't remember every detail of my life as a child. Some souls do, but I have a feeling I blocked much of mine out. Having been reminded constantly of my nightly wailing that went on longer than it should have, I wondered why I had been such an obviously nervous and frightened child.

It could have stemmed from the night my exhausted mother could not understand why I continued to cry when she was breastfeeding me. Then she realised that, in her stupor of tiredness, she had me upside down and was trying to push her breast into my toes.

(Soul note: Early signs of madness in this family?)

Or it could have been the fault of the dummy or 'comforter' they constantly pushed into my mouth every time I cried, then embarrassed me by pinning it to my clothes as a warning that, if I cried again, this horrible smelling rubbery thing was waiting for me.

(Soul note: no wonder my throat chakra was scarred, and tonsillitis came every two weeks till I was four, because I was never allowed to express myself!)

However, it is most likely to have been when my mum – young, vulnerable, and scared of the debt she had accrued, and which my father knew nothing about – fled back to her own family in Rothesay, Isle of Bute. I was left alone –just 8 months old, in my cot, locked in a cold room in an empty tenement, for a full day until my dad came home from work at 11pm that night.

He found a scared and hungry little baby, shivering and trembling in the darkness. A little girl who had no voice left after screaming and crying, when no-one seemed to care or come to her rescue. And on finding his child abandoned and just a note from his wife explaining that she had left him, his own life and marriage was suddenly flipped upside down.

Maybe it was on that day on my new soul journey that my fears really kicked in and 'issues' began to form in my now scarred little body. Emotions like rejection, unworthiness, burden, fear, being unloved, were terrible feelings for a little baby to process, but nonetheless these issues – without any doubt – settled into my cells and would reappear in many guises as I grew up.

I do have memory of this time, and can now recall it without fears or tears, and see it as an experience on my brand new soul journey; a memory. But for many years this unknown part of me created many issues within my life and I battled with rejection of any kind. I do feel that this abandonment and rejection by my mother – her fears and the issues it placed upon my little soul – set new neurological patterns in motion within me, and the effects would be seen, in time, on my own soul map.

My dad – a hard-working man – had been a professional footballer; he played for Liverpool's second team, and Scottish football teams, Motherwell and Arbroath. He had drive and determination, and was a talented man; a good sportsman, a great piano player and singer, and socially a popular man. It was while he was living in Liverpool that he met my mum.

She was a beautiful young girl from Rothesay – from a Stewart/Sinclair generational combination – working and training for the Woolworths' group as a window dresser. The combination of both their energies was, indeed, always part of my life. His fairness through sport, his team working skills, his attention to detail as a shoemaker, which was his trade, his willingness to work hard to achieve what was needed, his singing and love of music. Her flair for showing balance to the eye, creative attention to colour and design, how to make things look good when you had very little.

All these attributes surrounded me from an early age. I did not see this at that time, nor did I realise, as a child, that my mother was working through her own demons from her family, and my father his. They were actually amazing teachers on all levels. But when you are a child, you don't remember the real reasons why you came here, or that your soul came back here to explore more, grow and learn more. You have simply forgotten this part; you have made the trip through the veil of amnesia, and lost your soul map and instructions somewhere in the ethers on your way down to this planet. Your mind may have often wondered in those early years why God, if He loved you so much, would place you on a path where your soul would mostly grow through negativity like trauma, pain, fear, guilt, illness, addiction, even rejection, when all you really wanted and needed was Love!

I never realised that the mushroom method, growing quickly from a lot of manure or shizzle (my new word to describe all things that stink in life), would benefit me. That being left to grow in the dark, from the fear, was actually good for you! The fact that you could grow in many ways from this method, if left alone to expand in soul energy, escaped me. I was already programmed from that abandonment, and issues had started forming in my little cells. I simply was unaware of this.

When you are 8 months old, you simply require your basic needs met and be given lots of love. So when your mother abandons you in a cold, dark house in a creaky old tenement in the dead of winter, leaving you wet, hungry, thirsty, and scared to sleep due to fear of the unknown, of course your little life has been affected. My father was now the one looking after me, taking me to work every day to a very noisy, dirty cobblers' shop.

My exhausted father refused to tell anyone of his plight, because he did not want anyone to judge or criticise his marriage or my mum. A proud man, Dad did not want to ask or accept anyone's help. Intertwined in all this crisis, my absent mother was riddled with guilt, which was creating an even bigger chip on her already heavy shoulders. She could not come back because she felt she had 'lost face' with everyone! What a confusing situation for a baby to be in the middle of.

This confusion continued until 'Super Nany' came to our rescue and saved my life – and I suspect that of my poor Dad, too. Nany Kate eventually realised what had been going on once Dad finally reached rock bottom and asked for her help, and she immediately whisked me off to her little miners' row house in Newmains with all its unusual smells and strange noises. There, she loved and cared for me as if she were my mother.

(Soul note: this pattern of not asking for help, of being fiercely independent, became a pattern in my own adulthood. It is said that children are simply mini computers, downloading everything we see, feel and hear, with no blame, just recognition!)

That was the beginning of an amazing journey with this beautiful lady and, no disrespect to my own mother, Nany Kate was more than just a mother to me. She took care of me until my parents resolved their issues and I could return to a safe place once again. She showed me unconditional love every single day until the very last moment of her life on Earth. Even then, on her death bed, she showed and taught me unconditional love, respect, wisdom, and protection.

(Soul note: the term is Earth angel, a human who does not judge or interfere but loves unconditionally.)

By the time I was 3 years old, I was a very quiet, shy, nervous little girl, who spent a lot of time on my own, drawing, or playing 'mum' to my dolls when I was not in bed with infected tonsils, which appeared every two weeks.

(Soul note: definite throat issues and scarring due to blocked expression, as a result of holding onto the trauma of abandonment from earlier in childhood when no-one heard my screams! No wonder I was a quiet child.)

My mum dressed me in pretty clothes every day and I loved being a neat and pretty little girl. But heaven help me if I got dirty! There were always five clean frilly dresses displayed on the back of our settee, so that if I got one spot of dirt on my outfit, off that one would come and a new clean one put on.

I never understood this. It really scared me, and my growing imagination told me that bad things would happen to me if I was dirty!

(Soul note: Parents really can affect our conditioning in strange ways. To this day, I am always cleaning!)

I enjoyed my own company as a child and was shy – eyes always down – had no self-confidence, no sense of 'personality', and did what was expected of me for fear that my mum would either shout at me or run away and abandon me again. I worried that if she did, it would surely be MY fault!

(Soul note: This could be when fear of rejection and guilt issues really began to affect me, and then continued all my life!)

Patterns of behaviour were forming and becoming imprinted into my little body and mind from such an early age, but I simply was unaware this was happening on a deeper level. I often experienced awful dreams about being taken away by a huge fox.

(Soul note: Instead of fear, in totem medicine the fox is your friend, who can lead you to fairies. Although some would say now I am 'away with the fairies', their valuable medicine is being invisible, blending into the background, being still and quiet, and through practice becoming unnoticed!)

How true this was of me. Even in my dreams, my subconscious mind was showing me ways to blend into the background.

I would constantly wet the bed.

(Soul note: bedwetting can be about fear of the parent.)

And I'd wake up screaming in the middle of the night, looking for love in some way, searching for a reassuring hug. Sometimes, in this semi-dream state, for some weird reason I would think that I had gone blind.

(Soul note: this could simply be not wanting to see what is going on in the family.)

Maybe I was simply releasing my fears from this journey and possibly other past life journeys, because I cannot – repeat, cannot – even now, allow anyone near my eyes, and I hate being wet!

As a child, I could often sense other 'people' around me. Sparkles of light would surround me and I would become scared, but I was always told to stop being silly, that it was just my own imagination. I would often have a sense of being able to fly and truly believed that if I got onto our roof, I could fly like Peter Pan. Even now, I can remember that feeling.

(Soul note: Children up to the age of seven can be very in tune with other worlds and other beings, and these visions and feelings are very real to them. They are intuitive, which is a gift they should always be allowed to hold onto.)

I often knew 'things' would happen before they did, too, and could sense energy changing and feel the need to retreat. But no-one ever understood me. Today, I would be labelled a crystal or indigo child, and maybe, given the knowledge we have now for our children of today and what they are capable of, my life could have been very different. I never felt weird; I just felt different. It was only how other people felt or what they thought of me that seemed to worry me.

By the age of four, we had moved to a new house; a brand new beginning in a new council estate, with new neighbours and new friends. Life was looking up and becoming more fun. But with a bigger house came more responsibility, new furniture, things for the new garden – and my mum was not always the best teacher with finances. Her naive ways with money had been the reason for her disappearance when I was a baby.

Even after all that, she would still spend more than she had, and always in secrecy from my dad, then enrol me to keep her dark secrets. Dad hated debt with a passion, and I disliked keeping secrets from my father. She would have me waiting behind the front door for the post at weekends, in case Dad ever found out about her secret shopping. And lo betide me if I missed that postman!

So even from that tender age, fear was beginning to take hold of my little body and mind. Fear of money, fear of letting someone down, fear of loss, fear of separation, fear I would be a disappointment to both of them. And guilt, because I knew, on some level, that what I was doing was wrong. Yet, just doing what she wanted stopped the arguments or the thought of her leaving again!

Without ever realising it, I was being programmed to fear and have no respect for money. Mum's behaviour was conditioning me through her own guilt, which became my guilt; her fear inevitably then became my fear. Bless her, she never realised how this could possibly affect me in my future, or even at that time. All she was concerned about was hiding her secrets.

It is, however, a lesson for all of us on some level. Children are definitely mini computers, downloading all their parents' programmes. For their sake, make sure as parents that your own 'computer viruses' do not infect the programmes of your children! I truly wish I had understood this when my own children were small, and might have prevented them from downloading so much of my fear and ways, and those of their fathers, into their little programmed minds.

(Soul note: For those women who are pregnant, too, Dr Emoto Masaru has shown that water holds memory and, as a baby lies in amniotic fluid, the mother-to-be should allow her thoughts to be about LOVE, not fear. Be good to yourself and your baby, with words of love every day! I speak from experience, having had horrendous feelings of fear, despair, anger, frustration and more, during my times of pregnancy. Speak to your unborn child from your loving heart, no matter what outside influences are doing to your mind.)

I loved both my parents equally. Even at that early age, I knew they had both good and 'not so good' qualities, but my love for both of them was unconditional and never on short supply. I could see that, in their own ways, they both wanted the best in life for everyone involved; they just wanted it differently. They had different soul maps and read their own maps differently! If only I had understood that during all of my life until this point, my own journey would have been much. Never assume you know how to read someone else's map!

(Soul note: Fear is stored in the stomach area, creating an imbalance, showing up as lack of confidence – 'yellow belly', lack of self-esteem, running sacred of life, not standing in one's own power. This chakra, in my case, would be affected in later life with blockages, weight gain, and more!)

The battle to gain my confidence, to overcome my fear of life, the feelings of rejection, responsibility, and guilt, had already begun. My own little demons had begun to form, I was just too young to know or understand the effects on my life at that time, but the 'damage' and adopted soul patterns were already happening to me.

By the time I went to primary school I was still a timorous little girl. Extremely shy, I only spoke when I was spoken to, and did everything I was asked to do in case something bad happened to me. My goodness! At five, I had the responsibility of my entire family on my shoulders – or at least, that is how it felt.

I lived for a Friday. On this magical day my Nany would come for me; rescue me, sometimes. Every Friday, without fail, she would step off the same bus with an orange *(the colour of bliss, balance, emotions, and soother of traumas)* and a bag of sweets *(bringing sweetness into my life in some way),* and half a crown. Decimalisation had not been introduced yet, but to me 12p was a fortune!) This money would be put into my Post Office savings account on a Saturday morning, because I was scared of not having money. Look what happened when there was no money!

Nany would stay for her dinner, and then she and I would get on the same bus every Friday night and go to her house for a weekend of utter bliss, harmony, peace, and fun, until my parents collected me on a Sunday. Sometimes when she came to visit, I could feel the silence and even the tension building between her and my mum.

Mum could be strange at times. She was moody, and I could never understand why she treated such a lovely lady this way. I only found out later in life that my mum was jealous of Nany, because she knew I had this amazing connection with her and because Mum could not take responsibility for what she had done to me when I was a baby. I never knew what happened to me until I was in my forties, but the effects of that trauma had buried themselves into my cells.

Nany was a creature of habit; I knew exactly what would happen every Saturday. She would parade me about in one of my best dresses to all her friends on her shopping travels, and we would buy the exact same items every Saturday, from the same shops and speak to the same people. But to me it was never boring. I loved the security of the routine. These foundations felt safe; this routine made me feel like a princess, and not a problem. With her, I did not have to analyse moods, or wonder what was wrong, or what I was going to face during long silences or heated arguments.

Time in this lovely house was spent playing 'hat shop' or 'jewellery shop', and her bedroom was created into the most amazing play centre.

(Soul note: Through regression I have discovered I was a hat-maker in the early settlement times of America; a wonderful life, one of respect, creativity, love and fun. So maybe my soul was exploring those old feelings?)

Sometimes I was even allowed to empty her pantry and make a grocer's shop in the kitchen, and she would pretend to be my customer and would play all day. She had the patience of a saint. She would show me how to bake, and her home just oozed amazing love, together with that specific 'Nany smell'.

Papa – 'old Boab' – was an eccentric man, and had some very strange ways. But he loved me very much.

Nany would say it was my arrival that changed him, softened his hard exterior. I was so fond of him, but at the same time I was slightly scared of him especially when he came home from work and he would be black all over from coaldust at the pits. He spoke so loudly all the time, and always through commands.

I respected him though, and even as a child there was something that I deeply loved in him. In later adult years, I discovered he had saved me from a vicious attack by an Alsatian dog which tried to attack me from over a wall. He apparently stood between that vicious dog and me, keeping me safe and unharmed. I know now that this attack was the reason I awoke with night terrors disguised as that pesky Brer Fox, as he insisted on trying to scare me from that wall in my dreams. Thank you, Papa.

So here was a woman who gave me safety, loved me unconditionally, was proud of me, nurtured every part of me, and NEVER placed adult issues on my shoulders. And with her, a man who had saved me from harm. In their home, I was safe. I could speak and be heard, I could play and make a mess and express myself, I could tell her anything and she would listen, respond to it and accept it. I could offload and she would counsel me and I never even knew she was doing it. Everything she did was so natural, it came from her heart.

Kate always saw the good in everyone, even if, in my young eyes, they had done something bad. She was teaching me never to judge another soul. She went to church most Sundays, and sometimes she would take me. But when I think about her now, she was more a spiritual soul; she would say things that were different, and she was the epitome of fairness. I was grateful to her then, and I am grateful to her now. She was my strength; my teacher; protector; and she gave me an unlimited supply of unconditional love. She still does. For in my heart, she lives on.

During my early years at school I was an average pupil. However, if good behaviour earned a prize, I would have won that every time because I was always frightened of doing something wrong. Children were to be seen and not heard in my mum's book, but in fairness, she was only practising what she had been shown.

My mother's father was a handsome man. John (Jock) Stewart was a master painter and decorator and often worked for the Marquis of Bute on the island. A gentle, well respected soul, he had the waviest, thick, golden, coppery hair I had ever seen. God knows, I never inherited it! He had come home to Rothesay after he left his first wife Olive, in Canada, to return to his family's roots. There he met and 'married' Jeanie Sinclair. My Grandma, Jeanie, was a bonnie woman, but oh, so full of anger. I have never seen a picture of her smiling – always a frown, always angry-looking – but old Jock loved her passionately.

They had a 'common law' marriage, forerunners to today's 'live in' partners. This always annoyed her, and she had a massive chip on her shoulder, always feeling that folk were talking about her. She gave birth to my mum, who was born out of wedlock in the church's eyes but not in Grandpa's. They named my mum Elsie, after the midwife who delivered her.

(Soul note: is this where the lack of imagination stemmed from when naming me?)

Mum had a hard life with Jeanie. Her mother did not allow her to put a foot wrong, talk back, get dirty, be late, speak without permission, spend money or play before doing housework. If she did, she would be beaten with a belt.

(Soul note: I feel I can see a pattern forming here! This is the basis of how Mum treated me. Please God, tell me we don't have to become our parents?)

Mum was scared of her mother and had no confidence. Jeanie never showed her love, only criticism, judgement and anger, and she never encouraged Mum in any way.

(Soul note: A lot of this behaviour formed in my relationship with my mother, too. Can you begin to see and understand generational programming now?)

Grandma died when I was very young. It was a horrible, painful death as she was riddled with cancer, its acrid smell from its black poison oozed from her when she died.

(Soul note: Always release and forgive anger, frustration, and hatred of all kinds, as it can be related to cancer starting in the physical body. Do it now; right now! Let it go, forgive. For only love matters. Love is real, honest, true , and no-one dies through love!)

Mum escaped her island prison when she was 18 and went to work and train in Liverpool as a window dresser for Woolworths. That is where she met and fell in love with my dad, when he was playing football with the famous Liverpool team. At 19, she fell pregnant and, as marriage was important in those days, a wedding was quickly arranged. They tied the knot on 30th November 1951 – St Andrew's Day – and I was born the following June, just before she turned twenty.

She was repeating the same pattern as her own mother, and in the early 50s, the stigma of being pregnant out of wedlock was still difficult: the sins of the mother transferred to the child again. Like my grandmother, my mum always had a huge chip on her shoulder. In her case it was due to the patterns of her behaviour with her own mother. Mum liked to attack first and her moods could change the energy in any room. She seemed to feel punished, like one of life's victims, even when no-one wished her ill. She simply brought it on herself, and this became a pattern in her life; even as a child I could see this. She would nag and nag my father until he lashed out, then play the victim to get his love and attention, make him feel guilty, then she would feel empowered again.

She manipulated guilt to make her feel in control. I could see how this behaviour was wrong, on both sides. And by the time the 50s was coming to an end, I was more observant at the age of seven-and-a-half than most kids, who just spent their time playing! I could sense Mum's energy change and her mood blacken, so I would go quiet. But that too would be a fault, and she would scold me then plead with me to forgive her. She would threaten to tell my dad that I had been naughty, then hit me again. Then she would wash my face in freezing cold water to take away my red swollen eyes, due to the many confused tears.

I can remember sitting on our stairs sobbing, hoping someone would hear me and take me away from her moods. Then, out of the blue, she would hug and kiss me like nothing had ever happened, leaving me even more confused and anxious as I waited cautiously on her next change of heart. As I got older, she became more moody and temperamental. It seemed that both my parents were unhappy and the atmosphere was peppered with arguments, criticism, tears, rows, and blows.

Sometimes I enjoyed the weeks of silence that followed their rows, as no-one would talk. I would talk to Mum during the day and then talk to Dad after his work. Then, after eating in silence, I would sit alone in my room so that I was not seen to be taking sides.

(Soul note: Was this the beginning of my own issues with communication later in life, or was it my ability to try to see two sides of everyone's issues? Is this how I became a 'soul' counsellor, or is it simply paranoia? Ah stop, mind chatter;, STOP analysing my life!)

Sometimes their rows became physical and I would hear the thunder of voices followed by the earth-shattering silence after lightning struck! Time seemed to stop, like my heart. That eerie silence, that void of fear, crippled me and I would panic inside wondering what had happened. One distinct memory of a terrible row stayed with me all my life. There was shouting like never before, infused greatly by excess alcohol. I could hear them as I lay in bed, and I prayed that Mum would stop her incessant nagging, goading, egging my dad on, teasing him and generally driving him to the point of destruction.

It seemed to go on for hours in my little head – nasty, horrible words, swearing, throwing, and then... BANG, something hit the floor. And the silence that followed just about stopped my heart.

My dad came up to my bedroom and took me in his arms and said he was so sorry, and that it would never happen again. My mind was frantic; I thought this time he had totally lost control and killed her.

Then, as if emerging from the second blast of a dusty bomb going off, Mum appeared, her left eye so swollen and black it was almost invisible. My father, on seeing his damage, ran to her, enfolded her, kissed her, and told her how much he loved her and that he was so sorry. She said nothing, but just used all our energy to make herself feel in control once again.

Although I was worried about her and felt sad about what had happened to her, I was also angry with her. I could see that she, too, was responsible for this mess, and yet she had managed to manipulate the situation to make him feel guilty and her the victim. They did not think anything had harmed or affected me. They had no idea how frightened, how scared, how worried I felt, and I was sick of feeling this fear or acting like their parent.

And this pattern of behaviour became more and more common. Although I found solace in silence, I hated it, too, because it meant someone was hurt or was hurting. Their anger, their issues, their violence, harmed not only each other, but their innocent child, too.

I realised early on in my life that I would never tolerate physical violence. But no-one explained to me about mental and emotional violence; that realisation was still to come!

As you read this, I don't want you to think my childhood was all bad, because it certainly wasn't. My parents provided me with a 'good life' through their hard work. There was no excessive wealth, but we were comfortable, which was a balance in many ways. From an early age I was shown how to clean and tidy the house, wash and iron clothes, and sent shopping. I was a miniature mum. There were times when I felt I was disadvantaged, especially when the sun was shining and I was not allowed to play outside until my duties were completed, but she was just doing what she had been shown by her own mother and making sure that at 7 years old, I knew how to run a household. Quite the statement, don't you think?

I only became a child when I stayed at Nany's house. There I could go for walks in the Primrose Woods, play outside anytime, read, bake, and pretend play with her. And I am pleased to say that because of her, I do the same things with my own grandchildren. When they come to visit, mess is no problem, I want them to remember me the way I remember Nany. And as I write this, I realise that my grandchildren are actually healing me, healing that wounded little child within me, helping me find my inner child that went missing all those years ago through rules and patterns!

I do have many good memories during this time. We had wonderful summer holidays as a huge extended family to Whitley Bay or St Anne's, near Blackpool, which seemed so far away then and so exciting for all of us. There were no aeroplane flights, just bus journeys – Dad was the bus organiser, so I always got to sit in the front next to the driver! I would be so excited to wear my new summer dress and shoes, and carry my little bag with my books. Nany and Papa and my Uncle Sam and Auntie Teresa were all characters, and they made me laugh. I loved that when we were on holiday, there were never arguments, just fun!

For all their problems, my family had a great sense of humour and thankfully, this has been one thing I have always been grateful for. It certainly helped me through tough times! Laughter and humour help us lighten up, even when things seem bad, and it was a tool that I learned to use all my life!

As the 50s were coming to an end, I was learning to cope, learning to grow, learning how to please people, learning when to speak or be silent, learning skills on many levels, all moulding me into various 'ways' of conditioning; some good, and some not so good patterns, like fear, insecurity, lack of confidence, sometimes lack of communication. But when love was shown, when it was obvious and to the forefront, my life was good, it was happy, it was perfect. If I were to sum up this decade in my life, looking back at it now with these older eyes, it would be understanding how the patterns and programmes were beginning to form yet my little soul had no idea.

At nearly eight years old and a sole child, I was some-times lonely and craved company. Maybe the 60s would have more to offer my soul path in life!

Hindsight is a wonderful tool when used correctly. When we look back, reflect, and understand the jour-ney, we can forgive and can even forget. But as long as we understand it is always perfect for our soul, then no matter what is happening, how terrible life seemed, how badly put upon we feel now or have felt then, we can grow from it and become strong.

(Soul note: It is your choice, soul friend, as to whether you wish to read about this stage of alchemy now or at the end of the book; whether you wish to let the story flow, see it all unfold, and then understand it through the process of alchemy. I have to leave that choice to you!)

Chapter 2

Decade: 1960s

When 1960 came in, I was seven-and-a-half years old, still quiet but happy in my own little world. I discovered that I had a talent at school for speaking poetry. I was able, even at such a young age, to put emotion into words and my teacher always asked me to read for the class. I enjoyed this, as I knew I could do it well, and even now I use my voice to heal, soothe, meditate and motivate!

Around this time I have lots of memories of seeing 'sparkles' around me. I was always on my own when this would happen, or I would see 'faces' on the wall of my bedroom at night which would wake me from deep sleep! I know now that this was angels, spirit guides, and otherworldly beings keeping me company, but as a child I was confused as to why I was the only one who could see them. I tried hard to shut this ability down because no-one could explain it to me and it became frightening – until Christmas Eve, 1960.

I remember being in bed that night, so excited about waking up next morning and finding that Santa had been.

The anticipation of Christmas Eve is still the best part of this festive time for me. I love it more than the actual day, because it is the joy and excitement in souls that creates feelings of hope and wonder, love and peace that stirs my heart. It may also have something to do with what happened that special night all those years ago.

I was aware that Santa did not exist, Mum had 'proudly' told me so. But even though I knew this, my dad was wonderful at Christmas. Like me, he loved it and he was always the first 'child' to get up in our house! That particular night, I said my prayers Nany had taught me, and I asked for a gift beyond all measure. I must have fallen into a deep sleep as I have no recollection of the time I was disturbed, but I knew my parents were sound asleep, because the house was dark and silent when the sound of sleigh bells woke me up! Now, my dad loved Christmas but he never dressed up like Santa Claus, and there were never sleigh bells in our house. Yet this sound was so distinctive, as if I was in the middle of a movie, and I could hear this sound inside my room.

I remember rubbing my eyes to open them up. Standing in the middle of my little cold dark bedroom, was a cloaked figure, which at the time seemed so very tall, and even now, my memory would say well over six feet. I knew this was a man, not fat like Santa, but large, and he wore a cloak and held a staff. I could not make out his features or colours as the room was pitch black, but I had an understanding that this 'person' was very important. And he was standing in my room, silently, to visit me?

Other children might have screamed, but somehow I just knew that this soul was someone special and that I was perfectly safe, protected, and very loved! This was a meeting of hearts, and I had a feeling he was someone who would make an appearance later in my life. But for that Christmas Eve, something changed in me. I felt loved and cherished in a whole new way, a different way, and fear seemed to dissolve that night.

After what seemed a long time, he simply disappeared in a blink! Now many children have a vivid imagination, and I was a child with great imagination, but I knew that visit was real. And to this day, I can still feel that inner joy when I recall this memory.

(Soul note: Please accept your beautiful gift of channelling and inner knowing of all your senses, for many would have you labelled strange or, worse, mentally deranged. However, it is your complete connection to 'All that is', to God, and to your true soul essence.)

I fell into a deep sleep that night. And for the first time ever on a Christmas morning I did not want to get up, but to remain in my cosy bed, remembering my vision, my feelings, and my thoughts. Why did he visit me? Why had he come? Who was he? I remember eventually going downstairs that morning and just knew things were never going to be the same again! I thought about this warm feeling all day but could share it with no-one. Nobody would have believed me, and I did not want anyone to spoil it in any way! I just knew that day that something special was going to happen soon. I now had a true friend out there who understood me, loved me, cherished me, and was looking out for me. It did not matter if I didn't know who he was; it was my secret – until now!

As we recovered (and survived) from the festive season in our family, which always seemed to last for a week after New Year with our very musical family, I simply got on with my duties and my school work. I still walked on eggshells but learned how to navigate my young life really well. Weeks went by, and I noticed that my parents' consumption of alcohol seemed to be less than usual. As winter turned to spring that year, life seemed really good. My parents were unusually happy, my mother seemed to be glowing, and Dad was always so nice to her, helping her. It took a while for me to realise there had been no arguments for months!

In March that year they sat me down and told me the reason for their happiness. I was to become a big sister for the first (and last) time. I was ecstatic, to say the least. My lonely days would be over, I would have a brother or sister to love and maybe this would make my parents so happy that all the rows would stop. And it did, all the way through my mother's pregnancy; she was so excited to have this baby, but somewhere in me, I wondered if I would still be loved?

She never seemed to stop talking about the baby, and yet she seemed, in my young mind, not to include me in any of this. Nany saw what was happening and always made me feel loved. As the time drew near, I went to live with her again.

Looking back, I suppose this feeling of rejection seemed to follow me; I was being sent away again, and this new baby would have all Mum's attention. My heart told me, though, that it was going to be amazing having a new little friend, an ally in the family, and I was so excited when my little sister was born on 10th September, 1961, the same day Hurricane Debbie hit the USA.

Mum remained in hospital for a week, as the tail end of this hurricane hit Glasgow and our surrounding areas, creating massive damage and death as chimney stacks fell and buildings crumbled in the aftermath. I was old enough to become worried about my new baby sister, but I need not have worried. She was strong and quite capable of taking care of herself, as I was to find out in time. I remember my father coming from the hospital to Nany's house to tell me I had a sister, and that she would be called Catherine Jean. I recoiled because, in my young mind, she had the wrong name. My sister is called Cathie now – she was named after our two grandmothers – but at that age, it seemed a strange name for a baby!

She was born nine months after Christmas, so I knew she was my gift 'beyond measure'. And although she took her time in arriving, the lesson for me was that everything comes in Divine time! Patience has never been one of my great qualities, but I believe I was being prepared for her arrival by my very special Christmas visitor.

Cathie's arrival was lovely and I was learning to share my place in life with her. I loved her so much, but things did change for me, and Nany always sensed how I felt. A week after Mum got home from hospital, her own father died of cancer in Rothesay. I loved Grandpa, but I did not know him very well. However Mum was devastated, and she left with baby Cathie to attend his funeral.

Something stirred in me at that point, panic probably, for although I had no proper memory of her abandoning me nine years earlier, her leaving with this new baby to go home to Rothesay brought 'something' back for me and I felt rejected and abandoned. I kept asking why I could not go to my grandfather's funeral. I can see now, these were inner fears from that memory. They were not rational, but this is how our mind works. So I ask you now, please watch your thoughts because they can create feelings, emotions, and reactions which can either create peaceful and loving feelings, or total havoc. For me, my mind seemed to create havoc!

Mum eventually came home from Rothesay, and my little sister seemed to have grown into a cute wee bundle of gurgles. She was very beautiful and I always wanted to hold and feed her, but Mum would not allow that. She was so possessive of my sister. Once again, here were patterns of behaviour that were affecting me but which I just could not understand at that young age. It is strange for me, because there is a lot of Cathie's young life that I cannot remember, and I have put this down to being shut out from her by my mum.

In 1964 I left the comfort that was primary school to experience life at secondary school. I was twelve and yet I had to get a public bus by myself at 8.15am every morning to take me to school thirty minutes away in the next town. I had to begin to make new friends, which was a very difficult thing for me to do, as many of my old 'friends' had gone to different schools. In those days, our education system had three levels of secondary schooling. For the highest level of 'intelligence', there was a local six year high school and you were judged by one exam as to whether you were good enough for that school. Then there was the four year school for 'average pupils', which was miles away in another town. And then there were the pupils with the lowest results, who were put into a two year secondary school with a horrendous reputation. Your worst fear, when you were twelve, was being sent there!

My parents were so happy I was not going to the two year school! Me? I was disappointed that I never got to the top six year school! I knew I was exceptional in certain things, but I never excelled in main subjects like maths and science, and you were judged on your ability in these subjects then – and sometimes even today.

However, I went on this new journey and became more independent because of it. I felt very grown up travelling alone on the daily bus journey, being accepted by new people, and feeling confident choosing subjects I really liked, instead of being forced to learn others that I hated with a passion! Even today, I feel our education system has it all wrong – but that is another story.

When I reached secondary school, I began to accept that I was clever with words, good at languages, loved the study of trees and plants, disliked zoology – I could not bear cutting up any animals or insects – and I was pretty good at art. None of this pleased my father, as he wanted me to excel in maths and science but I didn't like these subjects. I excelled at French, German, Art, Geography, Botany, and was not too bad at English. When I look back now to this time at school, my soul really got it; my heart knew exactly what was important to me, what it loved, and to this day still loves. Even now I love nature, trees and gardening, the use of language in my work, and my creative side from art comes out in my home, my choice of therapies with colour, allowing that part of my brain and mind to be creative in everyday things. So I was choosing, in childhood, everything which would serve me in the future. The soul wins every time!

When I was fourteen, I moved to another new four year secondary school which was nearer home. It felt like a new beginning for me, and Cathie – now five – was just minutes away at my old primary school. School life seemed better, but life at home was changing for both me and my sister. I was at that awkward 'teenager' stage, plus I still felt 'different' to most other pupils. I was a bit of a loner, quiet, and I chose my friends wisely at school; I seemed to get on better with teachers! I always had things on my mind, while others were simply enjoying growing up. I was always worried about my little sister, life at home, doing my best, my duties, and everything else I was asked to do! I was an attractive girl, but always shy, never confident. So I enjoyed learning about 'how to look good' on the outside with clothes and make-up, and never went to school without it, even at that age!

(Soul note: Even then, I was learning to face the world with a 'different face', using this other face for confidence and gaining love and approval. Putting 'a face on' for everyone became normal for me as I grew older.)

During these times of change during our school years, things at home were changing, too. My father was forced to give up his job as a shoemaker, as being a cobbler was not paying the bills for his growing family. Mum had never learned about money and continued to spend more than her given household budget. Dad kept her purse strings tight for he knew what she was like, so there were still arguments over money.

This 'fear of money' logged itself firmly into my cells and, as I matured, I promised myself I would be good with money. I was a 'saver', and became adept at making things from nothing, like my clothes and personal belongings. I was not going to let Mum's inadequacy with money creep in and destroy my life; well, not at that point anyway! Mum's secret spending continued – and it had escalated. Cathie and I could never understand how our father did not see what she was doing. Why did he never question where all these new items had come from?

Now she had enlisted both of us to keep her secrets, and my poor little sister was already being groomed in the job I'd had since I was old enough to know who the postman was.

We both hated keeping secrets from Dad. He was a good man, a fair man, and Mum was her own worst enemy. As we grew older, Dad took on extra jobs to feed and clothe his family and give us our annual summer holiday. He also worked at weekends singing in local social clubs with his brother, Sam. The Wilson Brothers were quite well known in those days, as they were both excellent singers and musicians. Dad was an amazing pianist while Sam played the double bass and was lead singer in their band. Between them, they built up quite a reputation and their band was in demand.

Mum both liked this, yet hated it at the same time. She loved the attention it brought, the social side of life where she felt good about 'her man'. But then she would nag and nag him about how lonely she was, and how she was always left with us. Sometimes I missed my dad at weekends as I would hardly ever see him. I had also noticed that their drinking was becoming worse.

During the school week, when he came home from work at the factory, to help him 'shut off' he and Mum began drinking at night. I despised this, because I would be made to walk the 30 minutes there and back with my mother on cold frosty nights so that she could sneak into the snug of the local man's pub – where women were still not allowed to drink – to buy a bottle of cheap wine!

Every night without exception some sort of alcohol was consumed. Sometimes my sister and I were glad of it, as it could make our parents funny, or happy, or they would simply fall asleep and we could go to bed knowing there was not going to be any fighting so school would not seem so much of a struggle the next day. Other times, though, it fuelled their arguments, or Dad would come home so drunk from these social clubs that a riot would happen! Things were going from bad to worse for us girls. Our parents could switch off through their drink, but we could not; we were constantly on edge!

The need to use alcohol to relax and have 'fun' became a normal way of life for them. Cathie was growing up, although my memories of some of this decade became blurry for me – and I was the sober one! I was growing into a young woman now, with a 'good pair of Wilson legs', large expressive eyes, and a good figure! The only part that let me down, I was always told, was my hair! From my toddler days till I went to school, my mother plastered my hair with carbolic soap and sunk horrible metal clippers into it to make waves! She made more than these waves in my life, but my hair was ruined. It was never thick, never easy to work with, yet Cathie had amazing thick hair! She had not been subjected to the 'metal monsters' which I'd had to sleep with!

I tried all sorts of ways to make my hair look good – perms, lotions, potions, even Sellotape to create my 'Cilla Black' kiss curls at night, but it ripped my facial hair off every morning. Nothing helped my hair. However, my interest in how I looked outwardly became my focus. In my mind, if I looked good on the outside then all should feel right on the inside. Right?

(Soul note: This myth of image over substance was something I still had to learn! Always get it right on the inside, without exception.)

As we grew through the 60s, Mum became more complex. My little sister was allowed to do all the things I was never allowed during school holidays. Even at this point in my soul journey, I was still the one made to cook, clean, and tidy the house. Duties for me were not negotiable, and differences were becoming more noticeable as I got older, although that wasn't my little sister's fault.

Mum seemed to 'spoil' her more, and tended to reward her with food as her way of showing her love.

(Soul note: How many of us use food to comfort or reward the soul? Is it guilt, fear, is it emotions not being recognised, or the feeling that 'I deserve' this treat? And whose benefit or ego does it feed? Time to acknowledge why we reward ourselves and others with food on the soul's journey, for your soul does not grow through this habit, only your body and your waistline!)

Music was wonderful in the 1960s; I had discovered the Beatles, the Dave Clark Five, and yes, I had even discovered boys! I was expanding as a Soul. Not only were my senses expanding, but my body was, too. In many ways, I was turning into a differently shaped young woman, although I was never really encouraged to think beautiful thoughts of myself because that would me being vain, or 'big-headed'. Compliments were few and far between in our house.

Life at home was often strained – one day all was paradise, and the next, the rows would be cataclysmic. I often fell into the realms of despair and embarrassment as my friends and all our neighbours could hear my parents argue.

My sister and I became closer as we grew older, as we understood how important it was for us to support each other. Confusion was foremost in our minds as children, what could we do to make *their* lives better? The roles were reversed, and *we* always felt responsible for what *they* did. So to avoid the criticism or judgement of others around us, we became more and more dependent on each other's sanity, company and loyalty.

(Soul note: This is the beginning of how many souls pretend all is well, they 'put a face on for the world'! Remember that make-up? It becomes a habit, a way of surviving and coping, but can have far-reaching damage. And notice the use of words here! What can I do to make them feel better... Oh my, my 'rescuer' patterns were surely beginning!)

When I was fifteen, I got a principal role in the school opera, Gilbert and Sullivan's *Iolanthe*, playing the lead soprano, Phyllis. Phyllis was a gentle soul, caught between the world of the fairy and reality. That part felt real to me; life imitating art, as they say, and mirrors how I sometimes feel today! I had a great rapport with my French teacher, Mr Ferguson. A very large gruff man, he reminded me of my papa. He directed the opera and tried so hard to raise my confidence, as he had a soft spot for me. He believed in me, and although many were scared of him at school because he was larger than life and so strict, I loved him and he treated me like a daughter. I had a lovely singing voice, but at home it was never strong enough, never good enough, so the idea of my family coming to see our week-long school opera filled me with dread.

Mum came first with Cathie and my Aunt Teresa to see me perform, and she picked fault with how I looked and how I stood. Even many years later, she would make a fool of how I had held my hands on stage. Praise was not handed out often, because that led to being a 'bighead' in her book of life; as she had never been allowed to be seen or heard by her own mother, she did the same to keep me down!

When she criticised me, what did I do? I laughed *with* them at **myself,** even though it hurt me deeply inside! It became my way of dealing with life; a coping mechanism. I would make fun of myself as a way of stopping the pain.

(Soul note: I can still feel the pain of doing this, this was judgement of my soul, even by myself. Please encourage your beautiful children to be all they can be, because the lasting effects of self-criticism and judgement are hard to shake off. Be nice to yourself every day, in every way. When you are cruel to yourself, you are not standing in your soul power, or your true

authentic divinity. Instead, you create fear – fear of criticism, fear of not being good enough, fear of everything! And you judge your creator, too!)

Back to the opera. Instead of being the lead girl in this production as the beautiful shepherdess, I was slowly becoming one of her sheep! My cowardice in standing up for my soul was beginning to really get to me. This opportunity for my soul offered me growth, to be confident, to speak out for myself, to show what I was really like and good at. Alas, it all passed in a blur, like most of that decade.

I have to say that after Mum criticised and discouraged me during that week, I dreaded my father and my uncle – **the** singers in our family – coming to the show on the last night. But Dad was full of praise for me, and both he and Uncle Sam cried with pride. As a surprise, he had arranged with the school for me to be presented with a bouquet of flowers for my birthday, which fell on that night! I had never been given flowers before, or been treated so grown up by my father... ever. And my heart burst with great pride and great love, for this beautiful gift.

I still appreciate flowers to this day, and I feel it is related to the emotions of that very night! It is such a good memory of this time and, yes, I still love Gilbert and Sullivan to this day! As I remember that night even now, it makes me happy and proud of my achievement and hard work. I was so relieved that I had made my father proud of me, and life felt good – a glimmer of light and hope in what felt at times to be a very dark time for my soul.

By the end of that year, Papa died of lung and throat cancer. My poor Nany struggled to deal with his death, and after long arduous months of nursing him through his terrible illness, her tired body and mind seemed to fall to pieces and she took ill, too. She came and stayed with us for three weeks and it felt great having her with us every day. I so loved my mum for caring for her, and although she had issues with Nany, it showed me that Mum's heart was truly in the right place.

(Soul note: It may appear that I am constantly 'judging' my mother in my story, but please know, I am simply exploring how her energy, beliefs, habits, and her patterns affected mine from childhood. It is not about judgement, only reflection, to gain an understanding of my own soul choices. I loved my mum, and even now miss her dreadfully.)

My mum had a way of grounding her children. Not 'grounding' us for being naughty – we were NEVER naughty, the very idea! She felt it her duty to simply keep her girls' feet firmly on the ground to save us becoming above our station in life. God forbid if we ever got ideas of grandeur, or – worse – bettering our lives. That would never do!

(Soul note: I now always give immense encouragement and unlimited supply of loving words to children, and adults. All souls respond better to love than to judgement or criticism, and this allows their beautiful souls to soar! A good soul recipe is to take love from your heart, add unlimited belief in them, mix well with praise and encouragement, a spoonful of strength, and a sprinkle of honesty, and watch their souls rise into their own delicious masterpiece.)

Mum did things the way SHE had been shown in her life, and that is what happens in our genetic lineage. It was such a shame that she had never felt that deep love from her own mother. She had been constantly judged by my grandmother and put down on so many levels, so my mum was just repeating what she knew, what she had been shown from childhood. It was not her fault; deep down, I knew my mother loved us deeply, but she simply had problems showing it in different ways. Love you, Mum, always and forever!

By the time I reached year four at school –, my 16th year in life – I had discovered boys could be nice, and I quite enjoyed their company! I was a popular girl at school and knew that boys found me attractive, but when Mum found out I had a 'boyfriend', the restrictions came into full force! I was not allowed out on my own; I had to be home for nine o'clock; and everywhere I went, I had to take my little sister with me. Now, when you are a teenager, that is simply not 'cool', and resentment began to creep into my life. I resented my mother, even my sister at times, and I certainly resented the control over my life. Life was simply 'not fair'!

I never knew what it was like to have a proper boyfriend, as I was always afraid of my mum creating a situation, a drama, a mood, or even setting more restrictions. It was simply easier to not have one! So I spent my time studying for my 'O' grades and passed all six of them – English, French, geography (for which I won top prize), arithmetic, botany and art. Dad was so pleased with me that he went out and bought me a proper brown leather handbag. He chose it himself, something he had never done for anyone. Mum seemed very jealous of that gesture, and took the bag from me for herself! She told me I was too young to own a leather handbag and it was put in a cupboard, only to be used by her when she went out. I was so hurt. No matter what I did to please her, it always seemed to backfire on me.

As I had gained all my grades, I could now move to yet another school – the one I had wanted to go to in the first place. There, in my final two years, I could go on to sit my Highers in French, art, geography and English. I adored those two years, because I became a young woman during that time, one who made new friends easily even though I was the new girl at school.

I felt popular, was respected by teachers, and I knew how to make the best of my new life. Even though this was now my third secondary school, my confidence was growing, and I won first prize in both years for geography. Mum did not go to the prizegiving the first time I won, but she came to watch me pick up top prize for geography in my last year at school.

I had chosen two Collins pocket books as my gift – one on trees, and one on gemstones and crystals! I still love both these subjects, and somehow my soul knew then what would matter to me in my future life. Of course, Mum ridiculed my choices and said I should have chosen a novel she could read. However, I didn't try to justify my choice to her; there was no point. She kept at me, goading me like she did with my dad, but I quietly dismissed her criticism, preferring not to react to her insults.

Something changed that day, both in me and in her. Deep down she realised her daughter was growing up and learning not to react, to believe in her own choices, and feel proud of those choices. My confidence and strength grew against all odds, and life began to change. Life at home became different in some ways, because I knew I was able to look after myself and make choices whether Mum liked it or not. Seeing that she had now lost control of me, she began placing her control on my sister instead.

My parents' drinking was escalating by the time I was ready to leave school at the end of the 60s. Cathie was now nine – the age I had been when she was born – and she was dealing with the same issues in her own little way. She had really good friends and stayed at their homes a lot. And again, Nany Kate was always there for her just as she had been for me!

Cathie seemed okay in her own wee world, or at least, I thought she was. But just like me, she had learned the ability to keep a lot to herself! Our age difference always meant we were experiencing different parts of growth in life at different times of our separate soul journeys. However, as we grew older, we grew closer and would openly talk – we still do! – about the effects our parents' behaviour had on us, how it shaped us, and how we have grown from it all, rather than becoming victims of their 'stuff'.

Right now I'd like to say, well done, Cathie, for braving the journey with me and please know I love you lots!

(*Soul note: Always express your heartfelt love to those around you, because in doing so, their own heart and soul will sing along with yours! Even if you feel you are different from your siblings or family, be that in nature, ideas or attitudes, they chose to be part of your shared soul experience. Send them a huge virtual hug, right now, and they will know on some level. They will feel it in their heart and soul, sensing a huge ripple effect now as the love spreads and courses down the generations of time!)*

The 60s for me was a decade of learning to survive and growing into adulthood, which was tricky enough with those pesky hormones all over the place at times – most of them trying to escape through the molehills on my face! However, growing up with parents who abused themselves with alcohol, who abused each other and others with words and punches, whose moods became erratic and unstable, was tough at times. There were great times, though, like Christmases.

During all the years of my sister believing in Santa, I had learned to make things magical for her at this special time of year and this made me feel important and special, too. Through her, I was loving my own inner child once more. Summers were always warm, and winters were always snowy and frosty, so there was balance in nature, balance in learning, and balance in fun family times like New Year or large family holidays. Balance in these ways seemed wonderful, and when life was in balance, there was no fear; there was only joy, love, and even the freedom to express yourself!

When life was good at home, it was simply amazing. And although these two parents created many soul issues for their children, they still created much love.

(Soul note: This applies every day of your life. The balance of all parts of you as a soul with a body, brings great love, great freedom, and wonderful joy, so take time every day to centre yourself in love, from a place of balance, and create this amazing habit or behaviour to hand down to your beautiful children.)

There were many highlights and low points in this decade of life; the death of Papa brought about change – not in Nany herself, but in the family dynamics in general and also in her own life journey. Nany remained a stable source of love to all, and I made sure she was never lonely. She was my soul mate, my best friend, and my confidante, who taught me wisely that to simply listen to another but never judge, was a gift. She showed me how to understand that even if there were souls who criticised you, or tried to mould you into their way of thinking, it was still safe to be simply yourself, to speak your truth, and that no matter what, deep down they were only doing what they knew to be 'real' for them, they really did love you with a passion.

She was a truly amazing woman, a very special teacher in my life, and I am sure many of you have had such a special soul like her in your path, too! Treat them with great love, great honour, and respect, for they are worth their weight in gold! She was worshipped, not as God, but godly.

(Soul note: She was God, in a body. We all are, every single one of us, perfect and divine, but at 18 I had forgotten this part of my own soul divinity. I would remember again one day.)

So, back to the flower power 60s and the amazing music and clothes. It was a time which was a huge learning curve for me as a soul. I had learned how to find inner strength and resolve even when my heart felt broken, and it brought about an understanding of issues with alcohol, keeping secrets and guilt, the experience of both birth and death. It had been a decade which had fuelled my confidence and self-belief even when I was being constantly ridiculed.

On another level, my physical body and its developing chakras were definitely out of balance due to traumas, fear, and many other negative emotions surrounding them as I grew. It was a mixed-up kind of decade with extremes of great times, and extremes of low times at such a crucial age of development. And I have to tell you, I feel that many of my memories of this decade have been obliterated. The mind, unlike the soul, may have forgotten much of the detailed negativity, but the soul and its body stores it somewhere – as dis-ease, emotions we suppress, cell memories that can be triggered off in many new ways. We are simply unaware of this, because as children – especially in the first 7 years of life – we truly are those mini computers, downloading all we see, hear and experience, and programming our cells with lots of beliefs, patterns and behaviours that are learned from outside sources.

(Soul note: Never think that words or actions cannot affect a child, even if those words are not directed at them. They can absorb them as energy patterns and this energy can create much imbalance in their soul imprints, creating issues in their journey ahead. Always love, always from a place of love!)

The decade ended when I was in my last year at school, and yes, I now had a 'boyfriend' to boot! I was beginning to discover emotions of all sorts, I was enjoying these new parts of me, and I could see that becoming an adult could be just the ticket to a new way of life! For the first time, hope for a new future was beginning to become exciting, with new possibilities, new experiences, new adult ways of being. Life was beginning to take shape in amazing ways.

(Soul note: Remember what your mother taught you – never get too carried away with yourself, or get too excited about life, just in case it all falls to bits and you are left with 'egg' on that face! Better for your survival not to have dreams, for dreams can quickly turn into nightmares! Better not to have goals or ambitions, as you will only become disappointed and disheartened with life when they don't happen. Dear, dear, what had my life illusions become? My poor soul was battling not only my thoughts, and reacting to them daily, but now also my new found emotions!)

Check out the second stage of Alchemy – called Dissolution – at the back of the book, and addition of the element water which is connected to our emotions.

Chapter 3

Decade: 1970s

It is now January 1970, and in six months' time I will be 18 and ready to leave school and start a new journey in my life! My passion is to be creative and to teach children, yet no-one is listening to me as I near the end of my school life, even although I am on track with my qualifications. Somehow I am not surprised that neither my parents nor my 'teachers' hear me, because I am still struggling to speak with conviction, with power, and self-belief. I am still allowing so many others to take control of my life, and underneath I am angry, resentful, and remain trapped!

My boyfriend is a nice lad. He listens, I think? I eventually 'relented' and agreed to go out with him due to his incessant pleading, and the overpowering emotion of guilt if I did not become his girlfriend; that was something I could not live with. He was a popular boy in school, but really, I have to ask myself, Junsie, is *this* how you should choose male partners in life? Through pressure, guilt or *their* popularity? Confusion abounds on so many levels now, because I like him and he is nice, but why did I really agree to this? Was it the three P's? Incessant **pleas**, he was a school **prefect** (not perfect), and so he held **position** and was **popular**. Oh dear, typical of my left brain, that is four **p**'s, not three. My unbalanced brain is confused by my thoughts and feelings!

Actually, I lost myself in this new relationship. It felt like escapism and yet, it seemed more about his feelings than mine. I am not being disrespectful to this person, but although it was not quite right somehow I was reluctant to let it go, because he made me feel good about me!

(Soul note: You really were settling for second best, June! And really, did you think that looking outside of you would make you feel better about yourself? Surely not!)

As the start of the school year moved on, we were being asked what we wished to do. I had the qualifications to go to university, or teaching college then, and these were my priorities, but I asked my parents if I could apply to Glasgow School of Art. That may have been because my art teachers believed in me – unlike my parents! In their eyes, my art was terrible, I was rubbish at art, it was all 'rubbish'.

I even tried to justify going to Art School – as it was called then – to study Industrial or Commercial Art. These sounded more important, and I thought these titles would please my dad, but no way was he listening! I never even tried to convince my mother about it.

So I let go of art and thought, okay, I want to teach children in primary school! I applied to Hamilton College of Education to train to be a primary school teacher, because I loved the energy of children and the idea of helping them 'form' their little lives in a good and loving way. Why was I not surprised when my parents said no, backed up by an old school report which said, 'June has a very quiet voice, she does not appear confident. A very good and well behaved pupil, but maybe should consider another career.'

I was so angry and hurt that anyone, including my parents, had the right to judge me in any way, as deep inside I wanted to teach.

(Soul note: You should never allow others judgements of you – what THEY think of you – to take control of your life, or allow them to place their 'soul map' onto yours! What they think is none of your business! A lot to learn at this point, Junsie! Follow those dreams, have goals, be inspired, and be inspirational.)

Through various strained discussions, it seemed I was not allowed to further my education at all, as my parents wanted me to get a 'safe job' and earn money! Get to work, June, for in doing so your 'safe future' would be created!

*(Soul note: always listen to your heart and soul! ALWAYS! I allowed others to control me, make choices for **my** life, but this **was** my life not theirs. They said 'don't follow your passion, your soul choices', and I didn't! I followed their needs, their desires, their choices instead. I followed their soul map!)*

Having got all my qualifications now – 4 Highers to add to my 8 'O' levels – I eventually applied for a job in local government as a town planning technician, because some stranger told me that my success in achieving high marks in geography would be good in that sphere. What total rubbish!

I went along with it, which pleased my father and mother, as now I would be contributing to their income, their home, and it was a 'decent and good' boast-able job; none of that art school, 'druggie layabout type' rubbish in this household! Only solid, dependable, working class people stay here!

When school finished in June 1970, I was 18 years of age and excited about moving on. Dad got me a summer job to see me through the holidays until my real work in Lanarkshire County Council Planning Department began in the August, the time when the new intake of new school leavers started! School was behind me, but I was not allowed to take time out for just me, to relax and expand, to get to know myself after all those years at school. No, I HAD to work. Just as Mum had always made sure I worked through all my school holidays as a child, now Dad was making sure I did the same.

(Soul note: Life puts too much pressure on souls to be DOING life; we even describe ourselves by what we do, as if it holds rank over another. Remember, you are a human being, not a human doing!)

I went to work with Dad every day to Phillips Electrical factory in Hamilton as a summer 'temp' in their purchasing department, and I have to admit I did enjoy it. It opened my eyes and I actually grew, as a woman. I was able to interact with other adults, hold conversations, take instruction, and carry out instructions on all manner of new skills. Yes, I was still a people pleaser and did not want to let anyone down or look stupid in their eyes, but I was becoming more confident and my soul was definitely growing!

I had noticed new interest around me from the male side of life, too, but I was a loyal sort of girl, and my 'heart' would not allow me to wander. It was also good for me to see my dad in the role he played at work, because he was a much loved and respected worker in the company and everyone liked him. My heart would swell with pride when I told others I was Jackie's daughter! His insistence that I should work during the holidays was paying off, and teaching me some new groundwork in my own life.

Dad had won prizes for his innovative ideas to save this company money (oh that money again – one parent a spender, the other a saver), so when I mentioned his name, the reply was always positive.

(Soul note: our parents may have their own issues and can pass them down to their children, but we should always remember that they are on their own soul path. They can give us amazing groundwork for our personal journey, and also teach us their abilities of creativeness and innovation. So RESPECT where respect is due! Love you, Dad.)

It felt like a whole new world was opening up for me at work. I felt different, I felt strong and 'new'! I had new friends, new clothes, I looked different, and new possibilities were presenting themselves every day. This made me look at my then 'nice' boyfriend, and although he was a lovely person, I knew I had outgrown him. I wasn't 'in love' with him, and felt in my gut it was right to end our relationship but that was so hard for me. I had always been a people pleaser, someone who would 'go with the flow' to save hurt or pain, but although he had done nothing wrong, in my heart I knew he just was not right for me! I was guilt-ridden; I hated hurting anyone because I knew what it felt like to be rejected. However, I had to find the courage to end our relationship and I did. The poor soul was heartbroken, his emotions were raw and he tried so hard to hold on to me, but I just could not go on being controlled by any other force!

(Soul note: Sometimes it can be hard for us to follow our heart, and our mind tells us stories that can keep us in constant turmoil. But when we stop and listen to our inner voice of loving reason, and take action to simply do what our heart desires, we are taking an empowered step forward for all concerned. And even if not everyone sees or feels it at that point in time, we are assisting every other soul by giving them permission to follow their true path. Win/win outcome always with the thoughts of the heart!)

Making 'hard' (heart) decisions would become the way of life for me, and from this moment in my life's journey, the feeling of freedom to be just ME felt good! I began to buy lots of new clothes, looked more mature, felt more confident, and loved my new life. Would it last? At home I was changing, and although I still had my duties for Mum, I was learning to take more control in other ways.

Cathie, on the other hand, was not doing so well. She was now solely at Mum's beck and call and her ever-changing moods, but my sister was stronger than I had been as a child, and she coped in different ways. Dad seemed oblivious to everything going on in the background, as he was focused on his job, and thought he was teaching me great things by being part of my new process. In some way he was!

As I settled into work during that warm, sultry summer of soul discovery, my freedom was to be short-lived! A certain 'Tom' was about to make an impact on my life. He pursued me, paid me compliments, made me feel special, had lovely eyes and wrote me poems. What was there not to like? He seemed fun, light-hearted, and different to the last 'nice' boy. I did not want another serious relationship, nor to mother anyone or be controlled by someone else's feelings. Tom was not my normal 'type' of person, either. He was smaller than I would have liked, but he was a snazzy dresser, unique in his appearance! He reached my heart in a new and different way.

My dad knew I was growing up and accepted that Tom had a crush on me. But Mum was still defiant, did not support the idea of me becoming 'grown up', and still tried to control my life by limiting my whereabouts or how my time was spent with others. My dad won this time over Mum's over-cautious ways, and he accepted that Tom had an interest in me. So I accepted a date with this new beau, whose poem had won a place in my heart!

A date was arranged, but as usual Mum put on her own restrictions: be home for 10pm, no drinking, and no 'other stuff'!

(Soul note: People in glasshouses? Strange when some judge others or their choices, because when we do this, we see the mirror that is ourselves! I was not about to copy my mother's journey, to become her or wish to be her. She just needed to get

that! The truth was she was simply protecting me in her own way, the only way she had been shown! Love you, Mum!)

The date went well. Tom was the perfect gentleman, got me home in time, looked after me, and made me feel very special. I liked him, he was different, upbeat, funny and caring, and even although my temporary job was about to end and I was moving to my new job as a planning technician, I felt a new beginning happening here.

The 60s and early 70s were all about flower power, love, peace, and Woodstock. Those were the days, my friend, when feminism began, the gay rights' movement was launched, spirituality was changing. Looking back, all of that was amazing – the clothes, music, attitudes about love not war, many amazing things began to shape a new world, and many lives changed in those years. I was spiritually unaware then of how these various beliefs and 'new age' hippie ways were all interlinked and changing many souls!

My memory of this time was more about the clothes – the mini, midi and maxi; my amazing white patent knee-high boots; the many different hairstyles I had; my new taste in music from Black Sabbath to Abba, and my favourite group, the Beatles. Oh yes, to quote Mary Hopkins again, 'Those were the days, my friends!'

My favourite Beatle was always John Lennon and, although he was a bit unpredictable and unusual at times, I believe now I was tuning into his immensely wise soul, his insights, his energy, his skill with words and sound, rather than his personality or looks as a Beatle. He was a light warrior, and will be remembered for his profound use of words in his songs for many a generation to come. He was quite an amazing soul!

For me, this decade was about change; it was about growth and becoming a woman in my own right. I was not an extension of my parents' life anymore; I was separated from them, partly through some financial independence. And as I grew, I became more in control of just me, my own feelings, my own opinions and thoughts and my feelings about life. I had my own style, my own looks, my own mind, and my own job – and now my own life was forming right before my own eyes.

My relationship with Tom became part of this new life, and he became part of our family, too. I got on well with his mum and his siblings, although I always felt his dad had wanted Tom to remain with his previous girlfriend. She had been part of their family for many years and was also involved in their lives as a Highland dancer. His father played bagpipes for dance practice, and would still collect the girl and bring her to their house, even when he knew I was going to be there! I felt awful, really awkward, but Tom was strong. I was the one he wanted, and eventually life settled down and we all moved on.

(*Soul note: Here we go again – patterns, habits, behaviours, still trying to justify myself to others, to please others. I just wanted to involve them, love them, and be part of them. I simply wanted to be accepted as me. Can you see the many programmes I have running now? I had no idea about this at that time of my life, and although hind sight is great, foresight – and especially insight – is better. Get those inner eyes opening up, as intuition, inner sight, is our gift from God to assist us on this sometimes perilous and painful path.*)

Tom found a job with another council not far from where I was working, and began his own journey, learning a new career, so we supported each other.

He was always proud of me when we went out anywhere, showing me off to his friends like a prize possession.

(Soul note: This was what Nany had done all those years ago, so was I now enjoying this replicated feeling of security in my relationships again?)

To keep up this respect from him, I made sure I never wore the same outfit twice! *(Soul note: I wonder where this habit stemmed from, Junsie? Go back to childhood... and think! Oh yes, I remember, when Mum dressed me in many different outfits every day . My soul remembered that when you look good on the outside and keep yourself clean, nothing bad happens! My mother's conditioning in my baby years had possibly taken root here.)*

My life as an independent working young adult became focused on plans, savings, showing others how responsible I was, how I could be trusted and respected – and so there the patterns began again. Respect me with money, and I am loveable!

Cathie was now ten years old and beginning adolescence, that awkward time when our bodies, minds, and emotions can be out of balance. On top of this, she had to deal with home life more on her own, wee trouper! She seemed happy and we seemed to live different lives now, because I was working all day then out some nights with Tom. Yet she was still a vulnerable child and was dealing with her young life in her way, with parents who were now drinking more than ever. Her life was different to the way mine had been. Mum did not insist on duties and early morning rises so much with her – or so it seemed to me – but Cathy had lots of other 'issues' with our parents that I had not experienced at that age.

(Soul note: We have to remember that our mind map sees things very differently from another's mind map, so we should never assume we feel or know the same things. Your perception of someone's life may be completely different to how they experience it.)

As my relationship with Tom blossomed, he became more aware of what my parents were like and accepted that they drank, swore, shouted, and argued! He never judged me for their behaviour, and I trusted that he would not leave me because of their actions. A year into our life as a couple, Tom asked me to marry him and we got engaged on Friday, 13th August, 1971.

(Soul note: Surely our higher wisdom, our soul, SHOULD be aware that 'Black Friday' was not a great day to begin a new chapter? Was it an omen from above? Hello, June to Soul, were you blinded by love, or simply scared of staying with your parents for evermore?)

I agreed to marry him, and we set a date for 31st March, 1973. My focus was then completely on this new blissful road to freedom, a road that was taking me to a new place where there would be no house rules, no worrying about parents, no alcohol, no shouting. Oh my, such amazing possibilities were looming on that dreamy horizon. In my blurry vision of future 'Tom-land', I sometimes felt jolted into another reality by the way other people would question me, by asking, 'Really? Are you getting married to him?'

But I loved Tom unconditionally, and no-one had the right to judge me for the way I felt. What they were actually saying was, 'You are rubbish at picking a partner. You can do better!' So my soul set out to prove them wrong. I wonder now how I learned this trait, Dad? Maybe it was something I heard as a baby, a toddler – who knows? – but this was now a challenge.

To prove to those doubting Tom-asses, I focused all my energy into our wedding, which offered me impending freedom from parental restraints and others' opinions. I was totally oblivious to more 'new' patterns forming on my journey; I never knew I had this ability to shut out 'life' by making plans and creating projects. I simply got on with whatever helped me get through the journey!

As the whole family took on wedding fever, I realise now that Cathie must have felt very left out. Nany helped me enormously and listened to my insane babbling about dresses, food, money, and honeymoons, whereas Mum was just concerned about money as usual. Our families grew together, plans came together, and although Tom and I were together in many ways, I refused to be together 'that way' – if you know what I mean (blush) – until we were formally a married couple!

(Soul note: The fears and judgements of my generational past were affecting how I loved, and would love. There would be no pregnancy spoiling this wedding. I was going to be a 'good

girl' so that none of what happened to my parents and grand-parents would ever happen to me!)

Up to a point I enjoyed being the focus of attention during the build-up to my wedded freedom from life at home, but there were times when it really made me anxious and tense, due to my parents' 'ways' of dealing with life. I had finally taken time and choices for me in all of the madness, and one of my own choices was that of my wedding dress, which was Tudor in style, with long flowing sleeves and a Tudor-style pearl headdress that cut into my face like giant kiss curls (it was the same shape as my Cilla Black hairstyle from the last decade that had been Sellotaped every night to my now hairless face!). My birthstone was indeed pearl, so it seemed perfect. Looking at photos now, I can't help but think that all I needed was the tall pointed hat with the floaty veil and I could have been transported into the time of Camelot. But that's another story about my soul's past!

Eight months after I was married was the royal wedding of that year. Princess Anne wore a very similar gown, but I doubt if they were holding their day in the local community centre. Our wedding in March 1973 was ordinary by standards, but wonderful for our families, and everyone spoke of it with love, humour, and fond memories.

Dad was a very proud and handsome man, always tailored in his dress sense; he always looked perfect.

(Soul note: Oh no, could there be another source of perfection in our family I had overlooked?)

He was always very proud of his girls, and on that day, especially of his first born. When I came downstairs from my bedroom, all dressed in my white wedding dress, train, veil, and more, Dad never even looked at me. Instead, he kept checking his own appearance in the mirror above the fake stone fireplace, making sure I brushed any hairs off his morning suit, sprayed more lacquer on his now stiffly-groomed hair, and made sure his buttonhole was secure. Only after I did all that for him, did he think to offer a few words of praise for how I looked!

*(Soul note: This could be where my perfection issues stemmed from, always thinking it was my mother, when it could also have been my father. Or maybe it is my learned behaviour of making **others** look good as a way making me feel better about myself? A sign of things to come, perhaps? Don't we just drive ourselves crazy with our habits and patterns, and then so many thoughts about them all?)*

After a day of rain, hail and snow, we left our wedding reception as a happily married young couple, ready to embark on an exciting new journey ahead. That night, we drove to Glasgow and stayed near the airport in a high rise flat which belonged to Tom's aunt. She had 'gifted' us her home that night as a wedding present! How terribly romantic (I jest!), being in someone else's home, in their bed, on your first night as husband and wife – and what a cheapskate of a husband. I was really uncomfortable with the arrangement, but her offer had been organised by Tom's family so I went along with it, even although it was *my* wedding and supposed to be my special night!

(Soul note: Always ask for the very best for you and your life. You deserve nothing but the best! Follow your own heart

and not what makes others feel better about themselves. Learn to set boundaries; learn to say NO!)

The next day we were flying out to Tunisia on our first holiday abroad. Apart from never having flown before, I had never even been out of Britain! Although the idea of the honeymoon was exciting, I was nervous and a little scared as I changed into my formal 'honeymoon' negligee (my, how times have changed!) and waited for my new husband.

Tom was normally a passionate man, but for some reason he showed no interest in me and opted to sit up most of the night to watch television in his aunt's flat and read the early Sunday papers, while I silently sobbed myself to sleep! Feelings of rejection, of not feeling good enough, of being unloved yet again surfaced and, boy, did those tears sting! I was confused, I was hurt, I was angry, and so many other thoughts and emotions bubbled to the surface from my life at home. Here we go again!

*(Soul note: Now self-sabotage patterns are setting in – it must be my fault that this happened, I am ugly, I am unworthy of love, I am unlovable with victimhood undertones of 'why me?', why am I being punished? It **must** be my fault, and why is my mother's voice laughing at me inside my head on this night of all nights. I will not become a victim of my conditioning!)*

I woke up on 1st April – yes, you got it, another one of those timely dates again: April Fool's day – feeling like the biggest fool of all, waiting for the huge finger of shame to point at me. But really, what had happened the night before? Why had my special night been like that? Why had I been rejected yet again?

*(Soul note: Our mind has to make sense of others' actions, and so it will tell you stories! Please know that you are not to blame! So, if this resonates with you, stop self-sabotage programmes now before they become another habit. What goes on in someone else's head is NOT your business! Pay attention to **your** feelings, and **your** reactions to those feelings!)*

My adventures in hot and steamy Africa brought about sunstroke and swollen mis-shapen heads, fly-infested rooms, bites, and a constantly drunken husband. And I never thought I would say this, but I truly missed my family!

When we got home, we had to move in with Nany. Not the most romantic way to begin a marriage, but we had no home of our own as yet, and our parents had no room for us. With a spare room, once again it was Super Nany to the rescue!

Life was amazing for us in many ways, because she looked after us as if we lived in a 5 star hotel. I gave her money from my wages every week to help with bills, and kept all my savings in little envelopes behind the lid of the old piano in her lounge, adding to them each week. It's something I still do to this day. There was an envelope for our new furniture, one for carpets, one for savings, and one for clothes and essentials; there was no way I would ever row with my new husband over money. I had learned from the master of 'how not to do it' – my mum – so I was super-organised and in control of life. I was on top of my world!

Mum never wanted to hear about my honeymoon tales of Africa, she was not interested one bit. When I went to visit her with all my photos, after a few moments of silence she walked out of the room and into the garden, preferring to dig up weeds! Her silence and rejection felt icy yet again, so this time I simply left my old house without a goodbye and went home to Nany and Tom. She certainly had a strange way of showing love and interest in her children, but a part of me felt – and knew – she was jealous.

(Soul note: Mothers should love their children unconditionally, encourage them, and be proud of their experiences and adventures; so why would any mother ever feel that kind of emotion for her child? Deep issues here, bless her!)

Although the general mood at my parents' home was the same, some things *had* changed. While I was on honeymoon, they had replaced me with a wee green budgie called Joey. Knowing my fear of flying birds and flapping wings, I actually thought it was a deliberate way of making sure I never came back! At least Cathie now had a 'wee pal', and she spent lots of time with this bird, training him and teaching him to speak. He was a project for her, and us Wilson girls always loved our projects. We used them to focus on something positive, somewhere to escape to, to avoid having to focus on reality.

(Soul note: Watch this habit of blocking out what seems 'real', or painful in life, by investing time in new things, projects or others. Unfortunately those feelings and 'things' are still there, right inside of us, on some level! Deal with life, face up to what is ailing or hurting you, and speak about it, because it is creating an imbalance. Make it right!)

Life at Nany's was good but maybe a little restrictive for a newly married and 'so in love' couple, and at times I found Tom to be a little quiet. My gut feeling was that he was being 'secretive', particularly when I often found him downstairs in the middle of the night on his own for no apparent reason. One random day, when I was at home on my own, 'something' in my mind prompted me to search our bedroom for secrets. I had no idea what this feeling was, or what I would find, or where 'it' was hiding, just that 'something' was in our bedroom that should not be there!

My gut instinct led me to look inside our wardrobe, and then inside a box. Lo and behold, hidden under layers of various boxes, were 'porn' magazines. My stomach lurched; I wanted to be physically sick at what he had hidden from me. There were more horrendous books hidden under our mattress and on top of the wardrobe.

I sat on the edge of my bed, shaking, not knowing if it was with anger, shock or fear, but my heart felt as though I was being rejected all over again! Why would a man would lower himself like this? Why hide these horrible books from his new and loving wife, who so desperately wanted to please him? Why was this happening? Why would HE hurt me, too? Had I married the wrong person? My head was spinning.

I cried for a while, and then waited to confront him on his deep dark secret. There were arguments, long silences and moods. Once again, here I was, living a similar life to that of my own parents; my husband was lying to me and still making *me* feel like the bad person for going behind his back! This shook me to the core and was the beginning of many trust issues for me.

It took me a long time to feel 'normal' around him again, and my beautiful Nany gave me that time, never asking me what was wrong, just being there for me if I could not work through it. There was no judgement, no interference, just silent support and love for me.

(Soul note : Sometimes our wise and loving soul offers insight to the truth, opening up a path for honesty, openness, and communication. And even although the truth may hurt, know that it is always the soul's highest and loving intention to bring honesty into balance. The soul, your soul, never lies. It always wants peace and loving truth for you, because deceit, lies, and dark secrets hold no form in the soul. Following the voice of your inner wisdom is your strength and your truth.)

In time, we got a house a distance away from my family, but nearer to Tom's family and friends. And all my hard saving had paid off, as we were able to buy our amazing new and quality modern furniture with all my little envelopes! I loved this little piece of heaven and, living on our own, in our own space, meant we were very happy for a while.

Tom was a generous man, who could make me feel very special, and I KNEW he did love me deep down, but there was just something about him at times that I could not put my finger on. I was very good at putting a face on life for those around me, trying to appear to be the perfect wife. I was always immaculate, and my home was always immaculate, too; to anyone looking in, I probably had the perfect life. Yet that feeling of utopia kept escaping me. Maybe the damage from the early days of our marriage had left doubt and mistrust eating away at me from the inside.

Tom got on well with my parents, and socially he liked to drink as much as they did. It made him quite vulgar and loud at times, and his behaviour made me feel very uneasy, but my parents just laughed it off. I went along with the flow of life, as usual, ever the 'good girl', never stepping out of line, always the optimist, the one who would not put demands on anyone for fear they would leave or hurt me. Conditioning and behavioural patterns from childhood had already taken hold, deep-seated issues and programmes that I was unaware of at that time, but they were there, imprinted on my soul and my cells. And these patterns and programmes were affecting me every day.

We were not even settled a year in our little home when Tom was offered a job in London to further his career. Of course, he decided to take it without any discussion with me. I was simply to follow him wherever he wanted to go – like a sheep again – on his new path. (I knew I must have played that shepherdess in the opera for a reason!)

The move away to London was traumatic for me, and believe it or not, again I missed my family. Although I often did not like the way they could be or act, they were still my stabilising ground force, they were what I knew and had experienced to be my 'normal'. No matter their personalities and issues, I loved them very much.

I was a homely girl, so London life was not my cup of tea. During the initial move to a flat in Stanwell, Middle-sex, where Tom worked for British Airways, I tried to settle into my new life without family and friends around me. He was the extrovert, made friends easily at work, and went out drinking with them; he was Mr Popular, the new Scottish funny man – and I was his quiet, mousy wife. I found myself a job at the London Borough of Hounslow's planning department and began to come out of my shell a little, making friends of my own. In time, life did seem a little brighter.

Being in the silence of my own company a lot of the time, I realised my 'instincts' and hunches were growing again. I seemed to just 'know' things before they happened, but I could not share these instincts and feelings with anyone, not even Tom. One afternoon at work, I felt the urgent need to get home quickly. I told my supervisor I felt ill so that I could leave work, get on the Tube, and get back home.

Tom always had that particular work day off as a study day for his qualifications, so I knew he would be home; maybe there was something wrong with him? I got home to our flat around 2pm that day, but the door was locked and no-one answered, which was very odd. My gut told me something was wrong. Either he had taken ill or, worse, he was up to no good.

I battered the door of the flat so hard that the neighbour across the landing came out. I knew she didn't like Tom, so she took great delight in telling me he was definitely inside, because she had heard loud music just before I knocked on the door. I shouted through the letterbox that I was not going anywhere until he opened the door. About 10 minutes later, he sheepishly opened the door to me and I saw for myself the real reason for his strange behaviour.

My gut feeling added up to a girl from his office who was always hanging about, a messy bed, no sign of study books, and two very red faces! His pathetic excuse was, that he had fallen asleep, did not hear the door, and she was there only to help him revise but she had fallen asleep in bed. He insisted he had been asleep in the lounge. Now I may have been placid, quiet and, yes, even subservient, but what kind of fool did he take me for?

(Soul note: Ouch, yet again, my soul had guided me to the truth, and it hurt. And as tough as this was to accept, I now understand that my soul will always speak honestly for it has no judgement of good or bad, just truth!)

She left, promising never to come back again; he apologised and stuttered a lot. But it was too late, my trust was completely shattered. Tom tried hard to make me believe he had done nothing wrong, that he loved and wanted only me, but something in me changed that day. I still loved him, those feelings were still there –even when, months later, he almost made us homeless by spending our savings behind my back.

I had saved money and put it aside for the deposit for our own new flat! However, unknown to me, Tom had used it. So I had to rescue him again! For the first time in my life I had to ask for help with money. I explained the situation honestly to my dad and – bless him – with no judgement, he came on the overnight bus to London with the deficit and loaned us what we needed for our deposit. I was mortified, but yet again I simply ignored the issues surrounding me, thinking Tom would learn and change, and these issues would disappear.

At times Tom seemed so different to me. He was loud, brash, downright rude and vulgar, and I used to think he suffered from what some call 'small man syndrome'. Certainly, what he lacked in height he made up for in other ways, as he had to be seen, noticed, and heard! His ambitions seemed like lunacy at times and yet I was still there, still rescuing him/us, still loving him, offering a solid foundation for his life.

(Soul note: I had been shown these patterns of behaviour in childhood from both my parents; that it was better if you did not ask for help, for the fear of opening up to others meant that I may be judged, criticised, or – even worse – seen as a failure in their eyes. I never shared my feelings or worries with my family, because I feared –and those stories my mind told me – that others, like my mother or father, would take my problems, make them into their dramas, and then use that to justify more drink, more drama, and eventually more arguments. They would inevitably then blame me for everything, making my problems a million times worse. I was trying desperately to hold my life together on my own; what other option did I have?)

I carried on with life in London as if there was nothing wrong, watching him flirt with other women, and spend money for effect and for friendships which were all unnecessary. I knew he told stupid lies. But when life was good and it reflected back to me that man I had fallen in love with, everything felt right so I kept going!

I missed Nany the most at this time. I'd loved to have been able to talk to her about how I felt, without being scrutinised or criticised, or to have her famous chocolate cake or pancakes for tea, just even her hugs at times. Yet, on the other hand, although my time in London had been difficult and somewhat fraught, I had become a stronger woman for it. I had lived away from home, dealt with marital issues on my own, found work by myself, and matured in many ways. So this part of my journey was an integral part of my life, and my story.

(Soul note: Always remember to visit the past and see the good things that came from even dark times. Understand how those times helped you to grow and expand! Thank you, Tom, for pushing me to the limit!)

As my inner feelings began to grow, I knew intuitively something in my life was about to change. Then I got the news that Tom had been offered a job back home, in a town called Bellshill, Lanarkshire – halfway between our families – and a three bedroom house with a garden had been offered with the job, too. I was simply over the moon. Surely now life would improve and I would be happier, closer to family and friends again, and there would be *no more issues*. How naive we are at times!

When we got home after a long drive from London, having done the removal ourselves, I felt exhausted and not quite myself at all. I was happier on the inside but my mum thought I looked very pale. I felt she was differ-ent, helping me scrub and clean the new house, making lunches for everyone. She was being really nice and friendly to Nany, too, and we all seemed to be getting along very well. It felt so nice to have *this* new Mum in my life; maybe my absence had made her heart grow fonder.

(Soul note: Sometimes the way we treat others becomes a habit, too. Take time today to tell someone how much you love them!)

I had suffered a terrible bout of cystitis before moving up from England, and it was still plaguing me and causing me tremendous pain. The sickness was awful, and everything I ate made me nauseous! What a time to take a bug!

(Soul note: Cystitis, according to Louise L Hay's book 'You can heal your life', can come from feeling pissed off, usually at the opposite sex or a lover. Wow, that lady knows her stuff!)

I had been lifting furniture and heavy boxes, and maybe I was just tired, but I just knew something was not quite right with my body. As I scrubbed and cleaned, Tom organised the utilities. On the first night we moved into our new house, all we had organised was a mattress on the floor of our lounge as a bed, and a sheet covering our window as curtains, but I felt at home here and knew I would stay here for a long while.

That night I found a lump in my breast and the following day, as Tom settled into his new job, I ran to my mum, crying. She took me by the hand and then straight to her doctor, who examined me and asked me if I had skipped a period. Mum smiled, and I blankly stared at him, then realised I was indeed late. I was not ill, I was pregnant! Oh my, this was brilliant news; this was the magical new beginning I had been waiting for. Mum smiled for the rest of that day in a way I had never seen before. Her baby was having a baby; something was definitely changing for both of us now. It felt great, felt right, and everyone was delighted.

With pregnancy came an inner strength like never before. This little baby would be so loved and cherished, and no-one – simply no-one – would hurt him or her in any way.

Tom was loving and attentive for a while... until I began to look pregnant. Oh my, did that turn him off his now glowing and growing wife. He would not as much as hold my hand, show affection or touch me during those months!

(Soul note: Maybe this is why you always have to look your best and be perfect, as others will then love, support, appreciate, and respect you – always! Oh dear, my patterns and beliefs yet again taking hold in my head; those frilly frocks sure did have an impact on my little mind as a toddler!)

This was a time when I should have felt supported, loved, beautiful, and perfect, and yet I felt the opposite.

My baby responded well to my urgency to meet 'him' and he was born 'bang' on time; after all, it was Guy Fawkes' day. At 10.40pm on 5th November, 1977 my beautiful son entered the world, after a long labour. I was on my own all through this special time, which was quite symbolic, as that would be the way of my life for a long time to come.

So where was my dutiful husband at the birth of our first child? At home, throwing a big party and getting drunk. I was too much in love with little Scott to really be angry. I was just so content and relieved that this little boy was finally in my life.

My week in hospital turned out to be Tom's week of parties, and I came home to a messy, dirty house. There were cigarette burns on our new water bed and bed linen – strange, when neither of us smoked! I cleared up his mess, tidied the house, and set about life in my usual organised, perfect way.

(Soul note: Stop rescuing others, if they make a mess (even in life) then let them clean it up – on their own! How will they ever learn if you keep doing it for them?)

My little blue bundle of joy turned night into day; I was like the walking dead, as I never seemed to sleep. On one occasion, four weeks after Scott was born, Tom suggested he would get up through the night to attend to his son. As the crying continued, I cried with my boy, because I just did not know how to help this tiny wee babe. But Tom lost control, screamed at him to 'SHUT UP!', shook him, then threw him on top of our water bed. As his son screamed even more, through fear, I swore never to let Tom get up for him again. In that one second, I vowed my child would always be protected, loved, and that no-one would harm or scare him, especially not his father. That night, Scott and I began a journey together and our bond became very strong as he settled down into human life, and slept peacefully every night.

(Soul note: Dear Soul, were you showing me through my own child, how draining and worrying being a parent to a sleepless child can be? Maybe this is how my own fearful mother felt when she left me, her own sleepless child? The Universe teaches us in many ways.)

Scott was growing into a funny, happy, loving little lad and I adored loving him! He was bright and, like me, seemed to always sense things in different ways. I often found him staring up at the ceiling, or talking away to someone who was not there! He was 'different', just like his mum! I took comfort in this, and sometimes asked him who he was speaking to or what he was seeing. He would babble on about people I could not see, but I never put him down or told him he was being silly; I understood.

Tom moved job yet again, and went to work in Edinburgh every day. This meant he was out earlier in the morning and home later at night, so we hardly saw him. I ploughed my love and time into Scott and our home, always decorating it, creating new ideas, and making it feel warm and homely. While Tom worked away at his job, I helped earn for our family by doing skin care and make-up demonstrations at night, offering facials and makeovers to other women. I would travel to their houses and they would organise a 'house party' for their friends where I demonstrated and sold this beautiful range of skin care and make-up, usually to mums just like me. I surprised myself, because I turned out to be really good at it.

(Soul note: How clever of me – now I was even good at putting a face on others!)

I became a top seller for the skincare company, making a good income and winning prizes, including holidays. I really felt I was doing a great job, and my confidence and belief in myself was boosted. I took all the training I could get, and then learned to train others, to speak in public, and to organise large events.

(Soul note: Nothing is ever by chance! All this soul development was laying the foundations of my life to come. Look back

*at some of the jobs you have done – how did that work out for
you, especially now?)*

This was a job I could do with my little boy in tow,
which meant I had the best of both worlds. Tom always
seemed to be out, or late, socialising at the pub, but never
really spending quality time with us; it seemed like Scott
and I were a team, and Tom just joined in when he felt
like it.

I discovered that Tom's love of porn was back to haunt
me. And when I was 'told' he was visiting strip clubs in
Edinburgh in his lunch break and after work, that old
feeling from early in my marriage came back. The 'stories'
he made up to avoid telling me the truth always found
their way back to me. Truth, even if it hurts, always wins.
What a waste of energy!

While my marriage was showing cracks and felt
stagnant, other parts of family life seemed to go on. My
parents seemed to be living it up, always out at clubs,
drinking heavily and 'enjoying' their lives. Although
this did not concern me as much, because I had my own
issues going on, I was worried that my little sister still
lived in their battle zone of alcohol-fuelled arguments
and long silences, remaining in her room or staying with
her friends to escape the dramas. History was indeed
repeating itself.

Don't get me wrong, my mum helped me a lot with
Scott. She would babysit to let me work at night if Tom
was 'working late', and she would help where she could,
because she adored Scott, as did my dad and my sister.
Dad wanted to teach him football and golf, because he

had never been able to show his abilities in these sports to his own girls, so Scott was his new project and my boy looked up to his Papa.

Cathie spent hours with him reading stories or playing jigsaws. Mum gave him lots of Gran-love! On one level Scott seemed to have brought in new harmony, new ways of living and being, yet this wee boy also gave me a new warrior goddess energy, and I would have gone to the ends of the world for him. How life changed!

When the 70s came in, I had had a loving boyfriend who adored me, spoiled me and showed love in many ways. But during this decade, much changed too. By the end of the 70s, I had matured into a woman, got married, moved to London, got my own home, came back to Scotland to a 'changed' family, had a young son, and was a successful manager with a new company. It sounds quite a perfect life when written down, and yes, there were a lot of positive vibes going on. But, as this decade was ending, how did I truly feel? Did I feel the same way as when the decade started, with excitement, promise, and clarity?

Looking back now and reflecting my soul journey, I had never asked myself how I felt about **my** life. If only I had taken the time to face my truth instead of being programmed to 'just get on with it'. If only I had stopped at this point, as that decade ended, and asked myself: 'Does life feel better or worse? Do you still feel as loved, or do you feel less cherished? Do you feel secure in yourself, or does marriage make you feel secure? Do you plan for a future together, or is the future all about Tom and you are just muddling through, walking on eggshells behind him for fear of being alone? Who are you protecting now? And are you still putting a "face on" for the world?

Now, as I reflect back on my journey through this decade, life was still exactly the same. All that had changed were the timely goalposts and the people in my team. I still walked on eggshells – this time around Tom, instead of my parents. I could not make plans because I had none, they were just his plans; I never seemed to make life choices. Just like June the child or adolescent, my parents made my choices for me, they decided my career for me, they knew better. As for feeling cherished, that was soiled by a man who thought he was a man's man, who went with other women, drank, made rude jokes and jibes, would swear constantly, and generally spent his time with other people rather than his family. Other 'friends' got more of his attention than my son and me. No way did I feel cherished or secure, so what was stopping me changing this life? Simple. FEAR!

Fear paralyses you, stops the flow of endless opportunity, joy and peace. I was scared I would lose my home, afraid my choices would affect my son's life, fearful that my life as I knew it would totally disappear. I was simply not ready for that yet, and although my life could certainly have been better, it was comfortable. And again, when times were good they were great.

(Soul note: Why, oh why, soul, did you not see this repeated pattern of behaviour by now? Cycles of the same issues were stopping you from being all you could be because of fear and worry. But your soul will always see the truth; it is your ego, your mind chatter that works its dark magic. It was becoming a first class performer now!)

My issue was simple. I never dared express myself or speak my truth for fear that something bad would happen, so my mind was telling me 'better the devil you know'. Change is hard – what if you fail and prove them all right? It was better to live someone else's dreams, create and expand their goals than trust my own; better to pretend that all was perfect, all was normal, all was good. I was now protecting my son from harm in the same way that I had protected my sister in the 60s. The cycle of illusions, the lessons just kept repeating, and yet, I could not see this at the time. I was too deep in the fog, in the story that I was, in my mind's opinion, unworthy of anything better.

I had never spoken up for myself (Remember that big 'dummy', the repeating tonsillitis, and the little quiet voice?), for what was the point, no-one ever listened to me. I knew within myself that this had to change in some way, because this way of life would kill my spirit, and 'June' would simply disappear off the radar.

(Soul note: It can seem hard for many to step into your true essence, your soul. However; it only takes that one time to feel the surge of inner love and strength from your wise eternal loving soul, to want to keep changing. Alchemy might just be around the corner now!)

As this decade came to an end and I reflect back, I real-ise that my soul was kept alive by constantly reinventing myself and my surroundings. My hairstyles were varied and colourful, and my home was the same. I had become good at using colour and design-like symbols to create modern decor which was unique and often 'gossiped' about by neighbours. (Mum's creative flair taking hold of my spirit now). Tom had flair and style – I will give him that – and in some ways we complimented each other through our similar styles of design and ideas, even down to matching perms at one point. It wasn't my best look, and I blamed my poor mother for all my hair disasters!

I had begun life in 1970 as a single woman on a new adventure, beginning to feel free of parental restrictions. I ended the 70s as a parent myself, dealing with self-imposed restrictions. I was the continual optimist, constantly seeing good in others, always living by the book.

(Soul note: That Akashic book of mine has a lot to answer for! Think I must have wanted the most proper, pristine, perfect book up there – one that was never overdue, never damaged in anyway, and certainly had no dirty marks on it. I am sure the writing got top marks, too, and a gold star for effort. I had simply forgotten that God, or Creator – whatever you wish to call this source of love – had made me perfect anyway, and completely loved me just as I was.)

This stage of Alchemy is called Separation and, yes, I had separated myself from my parents during this time. But had I understood what this stage of Alchemy should be showing me? It should have been freeing me from self-imposed restraints, but as you read on, you will realise I simply could not read maps!

Roll on the 80s; life would surely get better.

Chapter 4

Decade: 1980s

Happy New Year!

1980 came into my life bringing hope, belief, and positivity; this was how I started every year! I would grieve for what had been, in fact I cried every New Year, and then quickly shake off those old memories and embrace a fresh start. I would be 28 this year and – looking back now – I was still so young, with everything to live for! My son, Scott, was 2 and a lovely, happy, clever wee boy. Tom, well, he was just the same, getting on with life and working in Edinburgh, still enjoying his 'man' time with football, mates, socialising at his local pub, and still the centre of attention everywhere. He was quite the social butterfly. That New Year, he suggested we should have an amazing family holiday to Miami in the summer. I prayed it would not be a replica of the disastrous one the summer before.

My 'job', although no-one seemed to think I did anything – after all, I was just the mum and not the 'main' earner in our family – had provided us with a highly subsidised villa in Corfu to use for two weeks! We decided to take Mum and Dad with us, and the saying 'NEVER AGAIN!' blasts into my mind even now. I was actually getting on with my parents, because Scott had created a new source of understanding within our family. They seemed to have a good life now in their own way, and Cathie – then 17 – was enjoying her freedom and friendships elsewhere, so all seemed peaceful on some level. However, I had not lived with them for a long time, and that took everything to a whole new level during that hard-earned holiday!

The villa rental was a gesture from one of the sales directors of the company I worked for. He gave me it for a small charge because I had worked hard, and I was really looking forward to it. I felt very proud that it was through all my efforts as a working mum, we were going to this amazing villa. I felt good inside, I looked good too – slim, very 'with it' fashion-wise, even my hair looked okay – and I could not wait to relax and enjoy some sunshine with my loved ones. Oh, how much did my soul not get that stage of 'alchemical separation' in the last decade? My mind or ego said this would be amazing, my heart wanted to believe my mind. My soul was saying, 'No, don't go, don't put yourself through this!' But it could not be heard over the chatter of my exceptionally great optimism (ego) saying, 'Go, it will be wonderful!'

When we eventually got to this Grecian villa – after I had to sober up all three adults from the plane journey from hell, and balance my child, his buggy, suitcases, and three drunks – first impressions of our holiday home was beautiful. The setting was simply divine, like the weather, and we had steps down into our own little part of the blue ocean that lapped below. We seemed to be at the very end of the island, as if you could go no further – and this sentiment brought about the same feelings with my patience and love for my family that year!

Tom struck up another 'new and *important*' friendship with a local bar owner, while my mother searched for Bisto gravy everywhere, to make mince and tatties! Dad just got drunk daily on Greek ouzo and floated in the sea, one hip up and one down in the water due to his recent steel hip replacement! A bit like my life – up and down, emotionally ready to drown!

Little Scott loved playing in the sunshine and being with his mum. Everyone else was either tired, hungover, or searching for Bisto to make mince and tatties in a country where the food was amazing! My little boy seemed to really love water, whereas I had a fear of it, so I had to rely on the others to take him in swimming.

(Soul note: I cannot and could not let go, because trust was an issue with this precious wee bundle. Trusting others to love him and keep him safe was hard - look what had happened to me! Why of why, did water scare me so much? Was this past life issues, or was it from the night at our swimming club when I was about seven and I went under the water, and not one adult helped me? I had been trodden on, kicked under even more, and pushed away; I had thought I would drown that night! It is so easy to place fear into our cells! Please, always remove fear from your life and from a child's life. Your fears become their fears, but can hopefully be their conquests! Don't take that risk:

always support them, shower them with confidence and self-belief.)

Dad had become a hypochondriac. Even as a child he was always ill, and this had now taken over his life. I have to admit that as a relatively fit man, to have hip issues so badly at this age was hard for him to accept, but he played on it for sympathy and attention. He had recently had his first artificial hip put in, which was one of the reasons – being the rescuer of the family – that I suggested he came to recuperate on this idyllic island holiday. What a mistake!

It became *his* holiday, and everyone was expected to run after him and tend to his needs. This really annoyed me with Dad, and now my sympathy was heading in Mum's direction. He was simply being a pain in the neck – probably the only part of his body he never complained about!

(Soul note: Hip issues, according to Louise L Hay, are about the fear of moving forward into important decisions, nothing to look forward to. My dad had THREE hip replacements before he passed over! So was he really happy on his journey through life? And was I repeating his patterns, his thoughts, his actions, by putting up with frustrating issues that stopped the flow of my life, too, and created blocks on my journey. He never spoke of his feelings to anyone, neither did I. I can see his patterns now – he'd just get on with it whether he was happy or not. Those hips told a story about his inner feelings, and yes, those patterns affected me as now I too suffer hip issues. All emotional issues can and will affect our physical body in time.)

On this journey through the 'Greek experience', we found a local 'bar' that provided meals. It was really just a man who had put up a gazebo onto his beachside garden outside his home; that was the extent of the luxury I was about to have on my hard-earned break. He served cold beers for the three amigos, juice for Scott and me, and delicious barbeque food with no Bisto gravy in sight! Service took hours, so we found ourselves there at 5pm for dinner, being served hopefully by 7pm, and in between much alcohol was consumed by those who felt the need. I was bored, fed up with this sort of holiday, and wanted to explore. Occasionally I went walks, just me and my boy, in his wee blue-striped buggy to get away from it all.

The holiday from hell showed me so much: my parents were still hooked on alcohol; Tom was still a philanderer and a flirt; and so life had not really changed one bit. I distinctly remember all of us being out at this 'local' and, Mum, Dad, and Tom stayed on while I took my child back to the villa in his buggy, along an unlit gravel road.

Eventually I heard my parents come home around midnight, loud and raucous. I waited, and waited, and waited, for my husband to follow them. It was 4am when he slipped down the side of the villa and in through our bedroom patio windows. I pretended I was asleep but he knew I was awake, yet he never spoke a word. Next day, I noticed most of our money, which HE kept in his pocket, was gone and that there was a strange-looking mark on his neck. I was devastated!

My mother knew there was an issue and, although she kept complaining about her own husband, I knew she was really trying to reach out to me in the only way she could. For once, I felt she understood me and felt for me, even if she did not know how to help or what to say to me. The holiday had been a mistake. It was awful, filled with heated arguments and icy atmospheres, and I vowed never to holiday again with my parents – and I never did!

(Soul note: Watch what you wish for, it can happen. Your thoughts are powerful and can create your 'reality'!)

Maybe this promised holiday to Miami at the start of the 80s would help erase these awful memories, and even be a great experience that would change us as a family? I was not a material girl. I appreciated if someone showered me in any way, but it would not buy me. So this had better be a holiday where it was heartfelt, soulful, and fun for both Scott and I. And guess what? It was! The day we all left Miami to come home, I cried leaving another country for the first time in my life. I simply knew America was my second home, my spiritual home, and that one day this Scottish lass, would return and maybe even live there.

Much of my story till now has been about my parents and how their ways, patterns, programmes, and beliefs, affected my sister and I. We in turn, learned to deal with and live through our own adulthood, working with and healing these patterns and programmes. When explaining my journey, I have not involved too many other family members or any of Tom's family, as they had not had the same input on my changing and expanding patterns. My own soul patterns, mind maps, actions, and reactions were already 'formed' as a result of my own family during my early years. These patterns and reactions were now simply growing due to my personal inter-action and journey with Tom. He had his own mind map, soul imprints, his own patterns and behaviours from his childhood and his parents. And there was no doubt now, we were not cut from the same patterns of cloth!

After our lovely family holiday to America, Tom went back to work. He always seemed to be working late, and my gut told me something was wrong with our marriage as he seemed distant and strange. One rainy Sunday, we went out for a rare drive as a family. As the windows of the car became steamy, I distinctly noticed a heart shape appear in the haze, showing his initials and the name of some other woman. I physically felt my heart leap into my mouth and began questioning him – as any wife would – about who had been in our car, and who this person was. I was told it was all in my head, my imagination, and that *I* was being unreasonable and stupid, as he blasted the car with air.

My way of dealing with this, as usual, was to go quiet, retreating inwards, worrying silently, and then convinc-ing myself it *was* my imagination, my fault. Somehow I managed to feel guilty. I never spoke of it again and tried to let it all dissolve with the other fears I had.

However, one day I decided to take Scott by train to visit Tom in Edinburgh, and surprise him at his office. As I stood in the office reception, I could hear them all whisper and glance over. Then one girl said out loud, "So THAT'S Tom's wife?" followed by more whispering and giggling. I wanted the ground to swallow me up at this point and could not wait to leave. My gut knew some-thing was wrong here, and I began wondering if I would still be with him if I didn't have Scott. I also knew that my heart's answer to my confused mind was NO!

I still loved Tom, though, and whilst love was still present, there was always hope that things would change.

*(Soul note: Was I stubborn, scared or plain stupid? Or, was it my **need** to be perfect at everything, including marriage now, that failure was never an option, so it was better for all of us if no-one would think badly of **him**. My head told my heart that it was best to love him unconditionally, that failure was unacceptable if there was still love in me. But where was the balance, the giving AND the receiving of love for my heart, my soul?)*

Tom knew things were strained in our marriage but even so he decided it would be a good idea if we bought our home as an investment for our future as a family. Looking back, this was both a good thing and a bad thing. This large purchase could become a financial noose around our necks and control our destiny as a couple even more, but on the other hand, it also gave me security as a wife and mum.

My heart was slightly concerned and yet my head said 'do it', as I desperately needed another project to hold this family together. Although the house was only £15,000 to buy from the council, Tom doubled the mortgage to £30,000, planning to use the extra cash for massive home improvements. Oh yes, we did love a project in our family! Projects take all our attention away from the actual issues affecting our lives. Looking back, projects kept me sane – my wedding was a project, my pregnancy became the same, and now this house was my next project. What I did not realise was that another pattern was forming, as

I was living through ideas, plans, and projects from my mind instead of simply living. It meant that my attention could be placed on something new, something exciting, something outside of myself.

(Soul note: How amazing is the mind! It is as if nothing bad happens while you are on a project, right?)

As usual with Tom, nothing was ever straightforward or 'normal'. As soon as we officially owned the house, he began making plans to rip it apart; he wanted this house to be the best in the street, the house that stood out from all others.

(Soul note: Remember, our personality or EGO mind. In this case, Tom's ego wanted to project out to everyone who he was on this journey; that he was snazzy and different, like his clothes, his hairstyles, his loud personality, mirroring to others that he had to be the same with the outward extensions of who he was, his material foundations, this home which had to be 'different'. It was about patterns again, but maybe his patterns. I was simply happy to own another home.)

He began designing this extension of his ego, which included not only a new kitchen – all I actually wanted – but also now walls were to be removed, a new hand-made spiral, wooden staircase built, patio windows put into a new dining room, and a new heating system which would be worked by an Italian solid fuel cooker! Then there was a modern log fire and chimney, which was to take pride of place in the new open plan lounge with built-in bar, new carpets, new furniture... the list went on and on!

I was panicking, because I could start to see this extra money disappear. And even although £15,000 was a lot in those days, he just seemed to spend and spend in his head! Tom had expensive tastes and was very flamboyant in nature, so I had to watch all his money moves closely. He had landed me in debt before with houses.

(Soul note: Will money issues never leave me? Fear of having it, fear of spending it, fear of controlling it, fear of losing it! FEAR – and obviously fear of money.)

By early December 1981, everything was legally in order financially, and ready for work to begin the following spring. Then the blow came. Like another one of those 'bombs' in my life, I was completely shocked and stunned when Tom was sacked from his job; his car was taken back with immediate effect and he was told not to work any notice. He gave me a lame and insane excuse for his job loss, which I knew was a huge lie, and to this day I don't know what *really* happened. All I know is, no-one loses their job with immediate effect for no small reason!

So now I was dealing with this new trauma, covering up some awkward questions from family and friends with little information from Tom, keeping all the stress to myself, stress of Christmas for our little boy, sharing my marriage issues with no-one. I never asked for help or advice, as that way everyone would believe all was perfect and I was strong, and coping amazingly well.

(Soul note: More patterns as I think back to my father and how he did the same when Mum left when I was a baby. For a long time, he muddled on until he finally asked Nany; he probably did this all his life, and just drank to avoid his own feelings!)

Money was simply disappearing as fast as it came in, and with the added pressure of a large mortgage to pay and Tom having no job to pay it, I had to step up and work harder to support us all.

(Soul note : I wish I'd known then that you, my soul, were always there, always speaking to me from my heart, because the silence at that time was so hard to bear. How easy it was to be lonely within a marriage and a family. Fear of life can isolate you from your one true friend – your soul. And yet you were teaching me, showing me, that I could survive on my own when I had to. I simply missed the lesson!)

Life was confusing, worrying, and difficult with Tom at home every day, and my little boy seemed to be influenced a lot by him in a worrying way. Scott would laugh when his father swore, and was becoming influenced by Tom's bigotry; he would react to his vulgar jokes, and like a mini Tom, began to copy his father's mannerisms. This was concerning me as I seemed to be looking at my family through very different eyes these days, and it did not feel right!

Christmas came and went, and I prayed for a New Year miracle. I discovered you should really watch your thoughts, though, because action always follows thought. And like the prayer I had made as a child all those Christmases ago, I discovered this time that the gift of life was coming to me. I was pregnant again, and part of me was so happy that a new little child was entering our world – a brother or sister for Scott – while another part of me was worried sick, as we had pressure from all parts of life.

When I came home from work at 10pm one night in that cold January in 1982, feeling horrible due to sickness with the baby, Tom told me an agency had offered him a job and that he had accepted it! I was so happy that God had answered my New Year prayers, even although I felt a little hurt that Tom had not waited to discuss it first. I was relieved, though, that it had put life back on track again.

Just when my soul felt relaxed: 'boom', and another bomb went off! This job was in Saudi Arabia and he was leaving within two weeks for at least 4 months abroad without us, leaving me to look after Scott alone and at the beginning of my pregnancy.

I continued working, which was difficult with no car and no-one to help watch Scott. Then 'boom' – another bomb went off! Tom proceeded to tell me that he had arranged for his brother to come at stay at our house while he was in the Middle East, because his brother's marriage had broken down and he had nowhere to live!

WHAT! Who did this man think he was making all these decisions without me – my parents? That is EXACTLY what they did to me a decade earlier when they told me what I had to do. To this day, I love Tom's brother. He is a lovely man and a good friend, but at that point – and he won't mind me telling you – he, like my parents, liked a wee drink, and now he was bringing HIS marriage problems, coupled with more alcohol, to my home. I felt uneasy. I had enough problems of my own, and what were my neighbours going to think of me when my husband leaves to work abroad and his brother moves in? That did not look perfect to that all-important outside world, did it?

I felt completely invisible in life. No-one heard me, saw me, responded to me, or cared what I felt or thought. No-one respected me! That night I silently cried, for somewhere in my heart I felt it was the beginning of the end of our marriage. Tom had clearly no respect for me or cared about what was best for his own family and I resented him for this. I saw a man who was excited about moving abroad to work, certainly not sad about leaving his newly-pregnant wife and son behind!

He made promises that he had only accepted the job with the condition we could all move out there eventually, but my heart was heavy with worry from that moment.

*(Soul note: Look at this! Learn to be guided by your heart and your strong soul. Just as my parents had made decisions for what **they** wanted for me, Tom was now doing the same thing; no-one was actually asking ME, what was good for ME, and yet I allowed this to happen again. It was my fault, my lack of self-esteem or belief in me, my inability to SPEAK UP for me. More patterns and programmes continued to take over my mind, more 'need to please others before myself' to gain respect and receive love from outside of me, even when my heart was shouting THIS IS NOT THE WAY!)*

Tom left, my brother-in-law moved in, and my life was horribly upside down. When my brother-in-law came home from work in the evenings at the beginning, he'd reach for a bottle to drown his own worries and heart-ache, but I was not having that with a little boy at home. I had been that child! And so, night after night, I would talk to him, and he eventually opened up to how he felt about his life, his own choices, about all that he had gone through and I 'counselled' him. I felt for him, because I could see bits of me and my life in him. No-one had listened to him either, or respected him, or showed him how much he meant to them, so he had been rebelling.

As time went on, his life began to change, and I grew to love and appreciate him like my own brother and great friend. He was so good with Scott, too. Eventually, he brought a new girlfriend to meet us and we all got on like a new little family. To this day, I love them both dearly.

(Soul note: RESPECT where it's due! Tom, thank you, for giving me this gift of friendship from two beautiful souls, in a weird roundabout way, who still show me great love, respect, and friendship and who will always listen to me and love me for who I am today.)

As months went on and my baby bump grew, Tom told us he was coming home for just a week around April, to sort out our visas. That trip home never happened; excuses were made and my little boy was very disappointed. The process rolled on till June that year when he finally came back with visas for me and Scott to return with him to this new land, new house, and new life.

Our house project had been put on hold until everything settled down, but at least we could pay our bills for the moment! When the time finally arrived for him to come off that plane, I was so excited to see him and show off our baby bump, yet he was distant, strange with me, even strange with Scott. And I remembered what he had been like when I was pregnant the first time. My body had changed and it seemed to repel him, but this distance felt different. Many months had passed between us, but surely he should feel the same as I did?

This time, I listened to my gut feelings and they kept saying that something was wrong. The plan was that Scott and I were going back out with Tom to Saudi Arabia to live as a family all summer in the new large villa his company had given us until nearer the time our baby was due, hoping that a permanent move would happen after the baby arrived. We said our goodbyes in Scotland and I left my home in the safe hands of my now happy and lovely brother-in-law to start a new family life in the Middle East. I was so excited, yet Tom was still distant. He hardly spoke during that long, eight hour flight, although he seemed to get excited as we neared the airport in Saudi Arabia.

We waited in this warm and strange place while our luggage was being thoroughly searched by soldiers or police holding guns. Scott and I were both scared, totally exhausted, tired beyond words, and all I wanted was to get to our new home and settle us all down for the night. It was well after 11pm and we had been travelling all day – but Tom had other plans. He decided he was taking us to a party! I hear your gasps. A party? At this time of night for an exhausted pregnant woman and her tired little boy?

When you are 6 months pregnant, the last thing you want to do stepping off an 8 hour flight to a new and strange country with a little boy is to go to a house full of strangers who had been partying and drinking all night. But there was no doubt this party was important to Tom, because he sped there, and all he could talk about was the people who would be there; strangers that I did not know or care about. He introduced me simply as June, and then dumped Scott and I in a corner of this stranger's house with some juice. We sat alone in that corner like idiots, invisible to all, and he spent the rest of the next two hours in the kitchen speaking to other women. One person asked who I was when I tried to get my son juice in this hot and clammy place, and I told her I was Tom's wife. A puzzled look appeared on her face as she repeated my words, "Tom's wife?"

At that point I simply knew my cruel husband was hiding something massive from me. After much persuasion from both myself and his tired son, he reluctantly left his 'new family' and took his 'old and now very exhausted family' home. We got to this large, now dark, house and found a complete mess. One of his 'friends' had got into the house and literally turned it upside down; quite the metaphor for my life at that point. They'd thought it would be funny to put all the bedroom furniture in the lounge and the lounge furniture upstairs into the bedroom, as a JOKE! It was no joke for a six month pregnant woman, who was now completely exhausted, scared as to what she had come out to, and totally disgusted with this behaviour. Where had I landed? What kind of people were these? And where the hell was the Tom I had known when I was young?

A few hours later, Tom was up early and off to work, leaving Scott and I totally upside down in all kind of ways. As the days passed, I began to feel a little more 'comfortable' in this massive three-floored villa, but I started to notice lots of weird things as I explored. There were hospital rubber gloves in kitchen drawers and bathroom cabinets, which I thought this was very odd, so I began a thorough exploration of every unused room. I found very small t-shirts in some of the drawers, hairbrushes which were matted with long black hair in bathroom cupboards; oh, how my stomach was churning!

(Soul note: When you see the signs, act upon them. Stop allowing fear to paralyse you into acceptance of what feels wrong.)

I did take note of all the signs; I noticed how he acted around us, how he seemed to never be home, leaving Scott and I in this strange country where women were not allowed to drive or even dress in certain ways. Life felt scary, and, again, I missed my family, my foundations. I felt alone, not only in my marriage, but in this strange land. I should have been enjoying my pregnancy, but I was too busy analysing Tom and his actions daily.

My days were filled with worry, fears, the 'what if' scenarios. Constant scary thoughts played around inside my head till it was ready to burst. Then, trying my hardest to put a lid on the thoughts, I convinced myself that *I was wrong*, that he would never hurt his family, especially here, when he knew I and his wee boy were cut off from all we knew. Under this huge emotional dark cloud, I had to appear as if all in my world was fine, so I acted as the perfect wife and mother whenever I was taken into company.

Apart from all his secrets, my worries, the long hours and the strange behaviour, I also knew Tom was involved with illegal alcohol in some way. And this worried me sick. Strange men came and went from our home, and they appeared to leave with clinking bottles in brown bags. He kept the 'Eastern toilet' in our home locked up, as it was never used by us, and he always had the key. I knew in my gut this was dangerous and illegal and I was scared. I would never do anything to put my son or my family in danger, but Tom did! I finally discovered that he was booze-running in the Middle East, and using Scott and I as his decoy. Unknown to me at that time, he was being watched, but our presence kept the police at bay.

On one of those low days, I called a friend back home, and for once I opened up and told her I was sure he was doing something behind my back. She then dropped the famous June bomb. While he had been home to collect Scott and me, he had boasted to her husband that he was seeing someone else in Saudi! My legs were like jelly; I wanted to be sick. I was sick! I had known it, but now I was aware of how this bolshie little man was indeed a liar, a cheat, and extremely cruel with it. He had brought me out to this mess and I was now all on my own, trying to protect my son from his illegal ways with drink, and now women. What a dangerous position to put us in; this was a Muslim country!

I challenged him and he denied it. Of course he would, he was a coward and he had got away with so much before because I had NEVER carried through on any of my gut feelings or accusations in the past! This time I began gathering information, questioning his 'friends', and as my appetite decreased through worry, I began losing weight in my pregnancy. I also noticed how his attention to Scott had all of a sudden increased, as if he knew he needed to have someone on his side. Scott always took his father's 'side', as if he was now closer to his daddy, and I felt so shut out of their men's club.

My senses seemed to be getting stronger. I began to simply 'know' and feel things again; one particular night I awoke in the early hours of darkness and simply 'knew' I had to search his car. As I opened the boot, I found another wardrobe of his clothes, including underwear, aftershave, razors, etc which he had hidden there out of my sight. I remembered sadly the memories of how my gut feelings had led me to take an afternoon from work all those years before in London and found him with another woman, and at the very start of our marriage how my instincts had led me to the porn he'd kept hidden in Nany's home.

Again my tummy threw a wobble of great magnitude. I squeezed my swollen belly into the driver's seat and instinctively opened his glove compartment. I found a card inside with his name on it, and inside was a poem from another woman. How ironic when it had been a poem from him that had melted my heart all those years before. She professed her love for him and thanked him for all he did for her and her family. Bile rose in my gullet as I sneaked my heavily pregnant body back into the house; his clothes now in the bin, I held her card in my hand like a weapon of mass destruction!

When morning came, I let him leave for work without a word, allowing him to make the discovery himself! He soon did, and when he realised he had been caught, he came running home to me full of sorrow and apologies, repeating that it was a huge mistake and it would not happen again. I had lost so much weight over those months in the Middle East that the baby clinic at the local hospital began to question me. I had a Turkish doctor looking after me here and he asked me one day if there was anything I wanted to tell him about my husband, because he was concerned about me. He wanted to know if my husband was treating me alright, as my baby's health was in jeopardy if I did not share with them what he was doing.

I nearly collapsed during this interrogation, but had the sense to say nothing. I had no idea how dangerous it was in this country for my son, or myself, if the truth about my husband came out. What *was* this man doing to us all?

(Soul note: God, when I came here as a good honest and 'perfect' soul, why did I choose people who lied, cheated, created chaos and dramas to share my life with? Would I ever understand this? All I wanted was a loving, peaceful life with souls who loved me and respected me. Why, God, are you doing this to me? Oh dear, that question we often ask our 'God', when in actual fact no-one is doing it to us; it is our acceptance of behaviour that is doing it; our fears, our patterns, our programmes that are creating it; it is our own ego that is creating it. God is simply still loving us, and our soul is allowing this experience to lovingly challenge and expand us. We just don't always understand that, unless we are soul-centred, of course.)

As I left the hospital that day, I went straight to the home of a Scottish girl's home I had come to know. She had been minding Scott for me while I was at the clinic, and seemed to look out for me. She knew what Tom was doing but did not want to be involved in his dramas, as he was creating a very dangerous situation in this country. When I told her what had happened, she explained that I was in danger, too, and suggested I should go home soon with my son, for all our sakes.

I was aware that she knew about this other woman and that the affair was probably still going on, but I was scared to leave. I thought that if I did, my marriage would surely end and I wasn't ready for that with a new baby about to come. So *I* had to fight for it – right?

My baby was due on the 16th September. But by August, between the booze-running, secret police watching us, affairs, lies, tears, and silences, I knew myself that it was time to leave. Tom booked a flight for Scott and I four weeks before my due date as restrictions for flying prevented it any later. That night, knowing he was getting rid of us soon, he threw a men-only party in our home with his 'friends' and, as I sat alone on the beautiful, cold, marble staircase, quietly crying and holding my baby inside my tummy, I listened to him laugh and boast to these strangers that he would be free soon because I was going home!

He broke my heart that night and, as I thought of my little boy sleeping innocently upstairs, I prayed for the first time in many years to God, 'Please get me and my children home safely, away from harm, somewhere we will feel loved and cherished.' I knew my husband, who had written the beautiful poems all those years ago, was not that man any more.

I left on a Friday and took the long flight home with Scott, my legs so swollen with fluid from the pressure in the cabin.

(Soul note: Pressure was something creeping in now, in many ways, and this was just the beginning of immense pressure. Please find a way to relieve pressure, for your body will only take so much.)

That night I called to tell him I was home safely, but there was no reply at our home in Jubail. There was no reply the next morning either, or during the next two days. I just could not get a hold of him and my gut told me something bad had happened!

Where was his concern for us, his family? Even if he did not care for me, what about his son and unborn child? Where was he? Who was he with? Oh, that mind pressure was now killing my heart and spirit. Tears flowed like a never-ending river and this intuition of mine was definitely kicking in, as my gut told me something was terribly wrong! After four days of worry, not knowing where he was, I got a call from his office to ask if Tom was now home.

I was shocked. As far as I was aware, he was there in Jubail at work. Thoughts raced through my mind. Where was he? Was he dead? Had he been jailed? Had he fled to another country with this woman? I was frantic, and my little boy could see what this was doing to me. He would cuddle into me and say, 'Mum, I'm here, don't worry, I will look after you and baby.' My brother-in-law was now worried and very angry with his brother; even for Tom, this was not right!

Next morning I received a call from an operator in another country called Bahrain, asking if I would accept a reverse charge call. After nearly a week of absence,

Tom told me calmly that he would be home the next day and would explain it all to me then! I was furious. I was bewildered as to what was actually going on in my life, and yet I was also relieved that he was alive.

(Soul note: always take charge of your own path, don't waste your energy on the paths you have no control over. Your path, your journey is the ONLY path that matters. I just did not realise that yet.)

When I met my husband at Glasgow Airport, I realised he had stepped off that plane with only the clothes on his back; there was no luggage. Then he had the audacity to offer me a bag of Arabic souvenirs! I never accepted them as I knew this was Tom's way of being everyone's best friend – the big man, throwing money or gifts at people to win them round. This time I demanded explanations. We did not speak on the journey home, as his father was driving – I did not drive then – and the two men exchanged banal niceties about the weather or the football!!

The story unfolded later at home. It would appear that on the very night I left to come home, as if to celebrate my absence, he threw a party in our house in Jubail and it was filled with many drunken expats. I later discovered from another source that many Filipina nurses from the hospital were invited, too, and right away I remembered the rubber gloves and black hair I had found in the house there. According to varied stories and sources, there had been loud music, flowing alcohol, and women; everything you are NOT allowed in that strict religious country. As suspected, he was indeed being watched by police, who knew my son and I had left, and had waited for their opportunity to pounce on him! He had escaped over garden fences and walls, crept about gardens until other people could hide him, and then lain low, hidden by folk he knew.

Someone had managed to retrieve his passport from work and then buy him a ticket for a flight to London via Bahrain. Our home there and all our 'possessions' – clothes I had left, all the new things for our baby, the crib, nappies, clothes – were now lost, money gone, job gone AGAIN, and at that point I wanted to scream, 'So is our marriage – GONE!'

His father came back to our home that day, unable to rest, and demanded to know what had happened in Saudi. Tom lied through his teeth and I sat there, sick to my stomach listening to this made-up story, because I knew it was all lies. I just did not know the full extent, the real truth of what had happened. His father kept asking me, pleading to know what Tom had done. For the sake of my child, and my unborn baby, I just kept saying, 'Ask Tom, your son is the only one who truly knows.'

His father came back to our home that day, unable to rest, and demanded to know what had happened in Saudi. Tom lied through his teeth and I sat there, sick to my stomach listening to this made-up story, because I knew it was all lies. I just did not know the full extent, the real truth of what had happened. His father kept asking me, pleading to know what Tom had done. For the sake of my child, and my unborn baby, I just kept saying, 'Ask Tom, your son is the only one who truly knows.'

His father dropped dead at work soon after, in fact, on the day my baby was due to be born. A few days later – my baby still refusing to leave my womb – Tom went to his father's funeral wearing clothes borrowed from his brother, and as his father was buried, I was taken into hospital to be induced. He never came to hospital to visit that night, and I was relieved that my son was staying with my mum. Funnily enough, I knew he would be safe and being loved there. What irony!

On the day my beautiful baby girl was finally born, Tom came to support me during her birth, unlike when her brother was born nearly five years before. There was a lack of nursing care that day due to a strike, but by hook or by crook, even if I had to go in and pull her out myself, I was making sure she was coming into this world!

Siobhan Kate Moore was born at 3pm on the 22nd September, 1982, and I prayed that day that she had come into her new world without the baggage I had been living with for nine months.

(Soul note: A baby in the womb can pick up on many emotions, not only from the mother but even what is going on around the mother. We now know that water retains memory, due to the fascinating work of Dr Masaru Emoto, and as the unborn child is lying in the waters or amniotic fluid, and each soul is approximately 70% made of water, it would seem probable that the feelings of the mother, and all around her, would affect the unborn child. Maybe when I was 'in utero', part of me had picked up on my own mother's issues and fears during my time there. Always love, always love!)

After I gave birth to our beautiful girl, Tom rewarded *my* hard work by tucking into my long-awaited toast and tea, then left 10 minutes later. That night, instead of coming to visit his wife and beautiful daughter, only my mum came bearing gifts. She asked me if everything was alright with Tom, because he was never out of the little office in the hall of our house, making calls. And if my mum answered the phone, it would be put down on her. That day she had heard him call and speak to a woman and tell her that he was a dad again, to a beautiful wee girl. My heart broke, because I knew this was the woman in Jubail – probably a nurse – who loved my husband, according to the poem she had written him. She was also the reason my husband had been run out of Saudi Arabia!

I thanked my mum for her honesty with me; that must have been hard for her. She was not interfering this time, she was just very concerned about her own girl. She always saw me as being strong, in control, my life always perfect, and that was how she had tried to bring me up, to raise me as a clean living, perfect child. I always did my best to carry that out, even when my soul was broken, my heart shattered, my mind in total chaos... So, yes, I appreciated her obvious concern and honesty that night.

Three weeks after my daughter's birth, I returned to work as no-one was earning and all the money Tom had made – and I had saved – from his Middle Eastern experience was now being squandered. As the past would reflect, we still had our house project to complete, and the money which was safely tucked away in a joint account was about to be explored. But surely by now you know the script – a project was looming, and Tom was bored without a job, so this project would save him from having to work at his damaged marriage.

He spent his days in that cupboard in our hallway, planning, phoning, and winding Scott up, while I was busy being a working mum, my weight now dropping off me. Months of this passed and I one cold, dark, January night I came home from work truly shattered and my brother-in-law, who was still living with us, was watching my baby girl, while my son slept soundly upstairs. When I asked him where Tom was, he shook his head as he told me Tom was out celebrating at the pub. I knew, I simply knew, before anyone told me that he was leaving again.

Tom came home, drunk as a skunk with happiness, and yes, he had indeed been offered another job in the same part of Saudi with another company, who guaranteed his safety. I simply smiled, too exhausted to care, and coldly asked when he was leaving. He never really answered, but went on to say that before he left us, he would order all that was needed for our house improvements, and organise the joiner and all the labour so that I could get on with the work here. I guess I had nothing else to do every day, that looking after two children, working most nights, cooking, and cleaning was just not enough for this woman!

There was a part of me that was so deeply sad that this was now my life, that a new little baby had been brought into what was becoming a one-person home and marriage.

However, I did what was right in someone else's eyes, as always; always the people pleaser, and always having a face on it for others; life was never about me. I was just someone's passenger and right now I was too tired to fight!

Tom left us again, and part of me feared if he was going straight to jail on arrival and that this job offer was just a ploy to get him back to serve some sort of sentence. Another part of me feared the pull to get back was more about this woman, and nothing to do with the job, money, or security for his family. He certainly showed no regrets about his past there, only excitement to depart again.

I settled into routine with my children – a single parent really – and when my brother-in-law got married and moved out, work began in my home, ripping it to shreds. Ironically, it felt just like my marriage, everything being torn down for something different to emerge and transpire.

Every night I sat on a small garden chair with a TV for company, no carpets under our feet, just bare floorboards. Every day I swept up dirt, nails, glass, and muck, painted and varnished, still trying to live as normal a life with a little boy and baby girl , before collapsing into one bedroom where the three of us slept. I even had to move out for a few days to allow the joiner to rip down walls, put in support beams, and make the new staircase. So my children and I stayed with Mum and Dad and, to be fair, Mum seemed much more interested in me now. Maybe it was my kids that helped this process, but right now she could see I needed her help, and she was a good gran to both of them. Dad, on the other hand, seemed to be drinking every day, and heavily, too. I noticed that Mum stayed away from him, spending more and more time alone in her kitchen, as he sat and consumed strong lager and cheap vodka.

I did not like my kids around drink this way and spoke to him about it, but he just laughed at me, and as usual I stayed quiet!

(Soul note: Patterns were still there, but changing all the time; pressure of his life possibly now hitting him, I just could see a changed man appearing from this alcohol-induced world he lived in, and I did not like it one bit.)

The work to transform our home seemed to last for months, and I was exhausted looking after two children – one of whom, little Siobhan, was constantly glued to my hip. I was working daily, trying to meet sales targets, cleaning up after the builders' mess every night, and I hardly heard from Tom.

I had noticed no money had come home or into our bank, and when I eventually challenged Tom, he told me there were problems getting his wages. Bills were mounting up, weight was again dropping off me, and no funds were coming in so the pressure was hitting me hard. For over two months I had not a penny sent home for me and the kids, and I was scared to even go for a coffee with my mum if she suggested it. I had put myself, my life, on a strict budget and I ate the leftovers off the kids' plates to save money. I was beginning to wonder if this was yet another lie; maybe he had been paid but his money for our family was going elsewhere?

(Soul note: I now understand how I felt 'not in control'. I was not eating, as that was the only part of me that I could control – oh my, deep issues forming now. And yet, although my gut was not being fed, at times it was keeping me right.)

After months of stress, and a near nervous breakdown due to being mother, cleaner, cook, project manager, worker, and balancer of life for all, Tom returned home in the summer to a brand new house – all completed by me, all perfect of course, for everything had always to look perfect ! I was good with interior design, so that part was enjoyable, but there were purchases which I would never have made, like the Italian solid fuel cooker – a waste of over £1000, as I had to stoke this massive 'cooker' up with solid fuel, or logs, even coal, just to cook. And it became unbearably hard to work with two little kids; it became out of control and unworkable – a bit like my marriage.

I have to laugh because, months after he had left to go back to his warm paradise, I received an airmail letter from him (no Skype or emails in those days); he wanted to send me extra money for the winter months. Nice of him, you may think. No, this was to buy a petrol-driven chainsaw for me to go out and saw down trees for logs for this damned cooker, to save *him* money! Tom was clearly living in some sort of alcohol-infused daydream, a bit like my father who was also increasingly becoming harder to live with or visit. What was happening in my world? Everyone was crazy, especially the men!

The visa to move out to Saudi finally arrived, and although I knew Tom did not want me and our two kids out there, I was determined to go to face the inevitable for myself. Money was not being sent home, so our bank account was in overdraft, and he had resorted to his strange ways of communicating yet again. This time, my purpose was not about settling out there as before, but to see for myself what the problem was in my marriage. I now weighed six-and-a-half stone, was skeletal-looking, yet I had this inner goddess strength, and I was about to find out just how strong I was.

I left on 30th November 1983, St Andrew's Day – also my mother and father's wedding anniversary – and all my family came to the airport to say their goodbyes. Mum pleaded with me not to leave, and both my parents asked me there and then if there was something medically wrong with me, as they were worried about my weight. My sister knew why I was going, and also why I was now so thin. All she said was, 'I will be here for you when you come back home.' And I knew she would. Now in her twenties, she was a no-nonsense kind of girl with a huge heart, and I had a loving ally in her. She was the only one I ever confided in.

Those words helped me more than she ever knew that night. With her, I knew I was not a failure; I was doing what I had to do to either reclaim my life, or create a new one! She was just like my Nany, unconditional and non-judgemental, and I was so glad to have her in my life. (Love you always, Sis!)

After a two-day, and for him, cheapest way expedition to the Middle East on my own with two children, via Amsterdam, the children and I were shattered when we got to the dreaded destination. Tom seemed okay this time and was attentive on our journey from the airport to the house with our children. Then BOOM, another one of those blasted bombs shattered the illusion yet again! Knowing his family were coming out to recreate the family life that had been missing at home and to repair some of the damage he had caused, Tom had now invited an English couple and their three children to share our home. I was completely confused, bewildered, hurt and so, so angry. He decided to tell me this when we were just five minutes from our new home. No wonder he was being nice to me!

As soon as we went in, their children were running amok in our home, the woman was in **my** kitchen cooking **their** dinner, and this strange man was watching **our** TV. I went straight to our bedrooms and unpacked, preferring to ignore these strangers. That was not like me one bit. Normally I would be a polite, interested, easy-going woman. *Normally,* but this was anything but normal! I was in hell, and so were my kids. I shook my head in disgust with Tom as I unpacked our clothes and got my children settled for the night. Deep inside I knew what he was doing, the avoidance dance.

These strangers were his protection from my inquisitions, possible rows, or having to spend quality time with *his family,* and I could see right through what he had tried to do. It was abnormal behaviour but it opened my eyes to a man I seemed to no longer know, and possibly no longer loved.

(Soul note: Dear soul, I was really beginning to find you in this decade. I can see that you were trying so hard to reach me, helping me connect to my intuition, assisting me with inner knowing and strength, and protecting me in many ways. Thank you! I love, honour and respect you.)

By the time Christmas in Saudi came, I was demented, and the only glow I had was from the fact that the other family was leaving to go home.

I found it hard to buy presents for the children in a Muslim country, and Christmas trees were definitely not commonplace out there, so it was something of a make-shift Christmas and I felt for wee Scott. I seemed to have made many allies by then – a lovely Indian lad who Tom hired to clean for us, loved the kids and respected me, and he looked out for us. He was called Lawrence, a real hard worker, and kept trying to help me and guide me; at times he would even 'suggest' to me stories about Tom.

I knew that on some level he was trying to advise me, and Scottish Linda was now a really good friend, again allowing me to talk about my fears. Although she did not want to get involved, I knew that she knew what was going on with Tom, and that this other woman was indeed still in the background. My Christmas gift from Tom that year was a multi-jewelled gold eternity ring. Maybe he had started to make an effort, you may think. But then, a week later – oh yes, have you guessed it yet? – that bomb exploded again!

Tom arranged a New Year's Eve party and, of course, being a loud and proud Scotsman, his party was going to be a proper Hogmanay night, so he invited possibly 40 people – all expats – to our home. Unknown to him, this was going to be my night too, as there was no way I was starting off another New Year with a lies from my husband. During the week leading up to this party, I became the private detective, something I had found a great flair for and would continue to have over my life. And I discovered that he had actually bought the jewelled eternity ring from his Filipina girlfriend to give to ME for my Christmas, but to also help *her* earn money! What a considerate man, eh?

One day I invited myself for coffee to another girl's house, something I was not really 'into'; she was the wife of one of Tom's drinking buddies, and one who I 'felt' knew this other woman. While there in her lounge, I asked her for a glass of cold water from her kitchen, which was at the other end of the house. I was finding my inner strength, and while she was out of the room, I spotted her phone book sitting beside my chair. I searched for and found the telephone number of Tom's girlfriend, who now had a name – thanks to Linda. This Scottish lass could see that what he was doing to me and his children was wrong, and she'd finally had enough of pretending about his lies. Just after Christmas, she had opened up to me and given me the girlfriend's name. So there, in this other girl's phone book, was the girlfriend's name, phone number and 'Hospital' written next to it. Rubber gloves danced in my head again! *She was a nurse*, and now she was about to hear from me, but not before I directed the floor show at the New Year party. Divine timing is everything; energy was shifting, and I was truly becoming empowered!

At midnight, King Tom was holding court at his show-off Scottish Highland 'FLING' (aptly named), when he turned to wish me a Happy New Year – in front of his grand court of 'friends'. At that precise moment, for the first time in all those years, I stood in my amazing power, did not react, but simply stared into his eyes. Then I said quietly, without a drama or causing a scene, "I know who she is, I know her name, I know where she works, I have her phone number – and our marriage is over!"

I calmly left the raucous party and went upstairs, where my children slept soundly, then walked to the bathroom where I had first found traces of her hair and hospital gloves. When he came into the room, he was shaking like a frightened little man, muttering all the usual words that truly meant nothing to him. I asked him to simply book a flight for me and my children as soon as possible; I was home within days.

My, how my inner power had shifted since the last time I'd left. This time I did not want to hear from him, and yet, he was the one never off the phone asking if we could speak, wanting to discuss things, apologising, and more. The balance had been tipped. And yes, at that point I should have called it a day. But not me, no, I had to truly GET it, so I took time out to *analyse* my feelings, to allow the anger to dissipate… and, when I felt he was sincere, I eventually allowed him back into my life.

(Soul note: Analysis leads to paralysis! STOP analysing with your Ego mind, and live from your heart and soul. When this happens, strong decisions remain strong.)

I went back out to Saudi the following summer with my two children, because I did not want him coming home. But this time I went out a very different person. Many of his 'loyal' friends said he had changed, that I had given him the fright he needed and that it had changed his priorities. However, that old gut of mine still did not trust him – and, boy, is my intuition good!

After a month of putting on a show, when I had taken note of a few slip-ups, like calling me by his girlfriend's name, it was time for my children and I to return home. I knew myself that I was alright with the decision to go home this time; there was no rawness at leaving him, no worry, not a lot of anything, to be honest. When I got home, as usual I called his office to let him know his children were home safely... BOOM! Yes, another 'June bomb' went off!

I was told that Tom was now on holiday for two weeks. He had jetted off as soon as we left – we could even have bumped into him at the airport, as he had left the same day – and was in the Philippines visiting his beloved, who had been deported months before the children and I had returned. Of course, that was why he had been on his 'best behaviour', because she wasn't there. No, she was at home in Manila, waiting for him and, wait for it, waiting for the heart operation that she so needed – which **he** was paying for!

And you, my soul friend, can now guess what came next. There was no money sent home yet again for his own children. Patterns had formed in my tolerance of others, but my soul was speaking to me directly now: 'Wakey, wakey, Junsie, is there anyone in this body? Yoo-hoo!'

That was a BIG wake-up call for me; that was the day I decided enough was enough. Tom tried his best to hold onto me and make me believe in him again, but my trust in him was now shattered. And in the cold light of this awakening , I simply did not want my children being influenced by a man who thought it was alright to treat their mother this way, to lie, cheat, swear, manipulate, and be selfish. No matter what, I would manage on my own, I had been on my own for so long anyway. I would work for my children and love them unconditionally, and provide them with a stable upbringing where everything was normal, open and honest, where love and truth would be in plenty of supply.

I began divorce proceedings to set my soul free of this man – a man I had loved deeply, but a man who had also made me feel dirty, stupid, worthless, pointless, and ugly. I vowed no other man would ever do that to me again.

The day my divorce eventually came through – years down the line – I cried, because I felt a part of my life died that day, a part that had begun with great promise, great love, and great adventures. But I was free now to be just me, a mum, an explorer of life once more. I took time out after my split from Tom to begin to get to know myself, to like myself again, and eventually I began to have a social life when Mum would kindly watch my beautiful children.

I have to say that, even although Dad was still drinking heavily, my mum was turning out to be a great gran and I completely trusted her with my kids. Now and then, they would stay overnight with her and they enjoyed this time out while I enjoyed my new soul adventures.

By the time Siobhan was nearly four, I occasionally went out with friends and enjoyed feeling like an attractive woman again. Eventually I met a man called Dick (I have changed his name, too, for many reasons. But you can see the Alchemist's sense of humour with names… Tom, Dick… hopefully Harry!).

Dick was funny, attentive, popular, and very different from Tom, and I was attracted to him in a way I had not felt for a long time!

(Soul note: I am SURE I said this about TOM, too.)

I really didn't know much about him or his background, but we began meeting for a coffee here and there and I grew comfortable with him. It had taken a long time for me to trust again, and just as I was 'falling' for him... BOOM! Oh, these bombs are going off more often in this decade than in the last one! I thought as you got older you got wiser, but what was wrong with me? I had allowed myself to become involved with a man who, unknown to me, was about to get married to another woman.

I was completely and utterly shocked, stunned, hurt, angry, and a host of many emotions all over again.

(Soul note: Why do all men treat me this way? Am I stupid, vulnerable, too trusting for my own good, and why do I keep making mistakes? Now look at what I am doing here. I am making this out to be MY fault! It must be me, I am worthless, I am stupid, and not loveable! STOP this self-sabotage, because you have been here before. He was the one in another relationship, not you!)

After the dust settled and I met up with him to ask why he had led me on, he explained that he felt unsure about his forthcoming marriage. There was a part of me believed him, because he seemed genuine and I actually began to feel sorry for him. But I did not wish to be the 'other woman', so I said goodbye and wished him well.

Although he did get married, within a short period of time his marriage was unhappy, by all reports, and he got in touch with me. I agreed to talk to him over coffee, and once again I noticed that he always chose out-of-the-way places to meet. What was he hiding?

There was something about this man I wanted to love, to rescue, perhaps to heal his pain, but little did I see yet another pattern forming in my life.

(Soul note: To feel good about yourself, you do not have to make others feel good about themselves. Allow their soul to work out their own plans, and simply enjoy yours.)

Little by little, Dick and I became closer. There was something about him that I was so attracted to, and I knew I was falling for him in a big way. For some reason, I believed his deep conversations when he would tell me that his marriage was over and to rest assured that he was leaving his wife. Eventually he did, and I was relieved for everyone's sake, because his tales of woe made his life sound like a nightmare.

He lived with a member of his family, who was also relieved that he had left and with whom I had become good friends. I got to know Dick and his family better and we all got on well. I supported him in many ways in those days – his work, his life, his needs and wants; I listened, I nurtured, I gave, and yet there was something underlying I just did not feel comfortable with. But I just could not put my finger on what was bothering me.

After some months of freedom from his marriage, he asked to stay at my house after a planned night out with one of his male friends. Although I was unsure about this, I agreed. When my children went to bed, I sat on my couch watching out of my patio windows for him to arrive, as I knew it could be late and I did not want him wakening them up. As I patiently sat waiting for him to come in from his night out, I noticed the red lights of a car

stopping suddenly outside. I went to open the door and...
BOOM! Oh yes, it was indeed another bomb; red was the
sign for danger now, it was his wife!

She asked to come in and I told her that my children
were sleeping upstairs, but as long as she was reasonable
and quiet, I had no problem talking to her. I actually felt
sorry for her, to be honest, and as she explained her side
of their story, I was appalled. Some of her story was new
to me. I had only ever listened to one side and so when
I heard her version, it confused me. She said he'd simply
walked out on her without any warning or discussion,
leaving her to fathom out what was wrong.

I explained that we were more friends than anything
else, but she had heard about me through gossip and
was simply trying to piece her life together. I was both
amused and amazed, as it seemed he had called the shots
in both our journeys. She asked if she could call him
from my house phone, and I was intrigued to see how
he would handle this dilemma, how he would react. He
answered her call thinking, of course, that it was me. I
would have loved to have seen his face when it was her
voice that spoke to him!

He did not come back to my home that night as
planned. In fact, he avoided both of us, not wishing to
face the fact he was telling both of us different stories. She
was fighting for her man and her marriage – just as I had
done with Tom – and all of a sudden I saw things from
a different angle. I told her to fight for what she felt was
hers, I would not be part of this, and he would no longer
be welcome in my home. There seemed to be an unspo-

ken bond between two women who both knew we were victims of his issues.

The next afternoon I drove to a member of his family's house to chat about the situation, but saw his wife's car in their driveway. So I simply backed out of the drive and went home. Now I was being seen as the other woman, the coward, and I simply could not be part of deception any longer.

I was later criticised for doing this, as his family told me I should have stood my ground. But I felt that both she and I had been through enough. After all, I had been where she was now; I had been that betrayed woman!

Dick went back to his wife after that, and I stayed away but kept in touch with his family. Within about 6 months, he had left again. He was still confused, still unsure what he wanted, or who he wanted, and this behaviour was about to become repeated over and over again like an ugly Paisley pattern in his soul journey.

He eventually left the marriage and, as 'fate' would have it, we finally got together as a couple and life seemed good. We were never seen as a couple in public together, though, and my instincts told me that it wasn't right to keep me 'hidden' so that his ex would not be hurt. My self-esteem was dwindling, too. My once confident self was now always apologising, and I felt guilty; it began to feel unnatural for me to act this way.

Something in me just knew things were being hidden, but on the face of it he had this ability to make me believe he was an honest, open, funny, caring man – so it must have been my paranoid self causing the problems. Oh my, had I a lot to learn about the men I drew into my life!

Dick eventually got his own place – a property that was tied up to his business. In time, he began to stay at my home more often, getting to know my children. But there **were** times when I truly did wonder what he did at weekends, and often he would be 'too busy' to even come for dinner during the week. I could write a book about the many times he stood me up; once I was all dressed in my LBD with my stockings, high heels –very Fifty Shades of Black – his special dinner all ready for Valentine's night, and he eventually appeared at 10pm with a family member in tow, to save his face! Oh yes, many tales have been missed out from this soul story, but that one deserves to be acknowledged. I could never understand why any man would do that.

He had got into the habit of coming over after five-a-side football every Wednesday night, and dinner would be ready for him. But for a few weeks I noticed that he seemed to have an excuse not to visit. That old feeling in my gut told me something was wrong and – ever the soul detective now – I had picked up on a comment from one of his work colleagues one day who'd mentioned that he'd seen his car in a neighbouring town when he thought he was visiting me!

I know now that this lovely man, who was such a good friend then, had deliberately questioned him in front of me, because he knew exactly what was going on. He did not like what Dick was doing to me and my children, and had hoped that I was smart enough that I would indeed pick up on this!

In brief, I *had* picked up on it. It turned out that Dick was seeing someone else – a girl whose mother was dying of cancer at the time, and he was offering her a shoulder to cry on, being her knight in shining armour. I eventually confronted her, but by then he was completely smitten. When she realised we were a couple, she took a step back from him. Once again he' been found out, and I was in the same position as his wife had been when she confronted me; it was turning out to be the polar opposite of my own marriage. Lessons were being shown to me, roles were reversed and being explored by my soul!

Patterns, habits, karma – no matter what you call it, this felt like my past coming back to haunt me. But this time, I **was** going to win. I had lost before, but not this time around. Do not surrender, was my motto.

(Soul note: Oh, Ego, you really were amazing, you were like the sly, cunning fox who sneaked up on me without knowing, creeping around in the darkness of my mind, in my dreams, frightening me into believing all was going to be alright. Fight to the end, never surrender, for you, JUNE, you are/were ever so wise and strong. You simply **cannot** *fail again!)*

I was so intent on winning my man that I never stopped to see what kind of person he could be; he had lied to me, and cheated on both me and his wife. I was fighting for the 'story', the drama, the 'but what if' scenario that played inside my head daily, when I should have been looking at the person; I should have been truly listening to ME, my heart and soul. However, I was not one for being beaten; look how long it had taken me to give in before!

By the time the end of the 80s came, he was well and truly my 'drug', and I could not function without him.

My love was so strong for **him,** but my 'self love' was gone. This man, in the space of a few short years, was my addiction; I loved his 'good' side, his funny side, his generous and loving side; I even loved him when he no longer 'fancied me. I loved him when I felt unlovable and had no love for my own self. I felt sorry for him, rescued him, made excuses for him, always wishing to make him feel loved in other ways, always boosting his confidence, always trying to make his life comfortable, successful, and always perfect! I was rescuing this person to the detriment of my soul – and his, too!!

I was 38 by then, facing middle age, with two children, and an ex-husband living in the Middle East, this time with another nurse – one he married within two weeks of our divorce! So my Ego told my soul at this point that this was as good as life might get for me, and to just 'work at it'. I was getting too old to change partners again, wasn't it? So put up, and shut up! Was my life journey about to change in the 90s? All I can say is, where, oh where, did my soul go?

The 80s had some amazing moments – the birth of my beautiful daughter, Siobhan, who just fills me with pride and unconditional love daily; the joy of seeing my son grow and develop into a beautiful, handsome boy; my marriage sadly ended; a new relationship began; and, in between, I was trying so hard to find 'just me'! Who was I? What was I? Who did I want to be? And what did I want to be? I also noticed there were no 'feelings' about me – June, the person – other than that externally I 'looked' quite hot in the 80s! I really did not know who I truly was on the inside at that time. I was consumed by those around me, things around me, situations around me; I was not 'at one' with me!

This part of my experience was all about my Ego, my image, how I was seen to be on the outside of my journey. I was successful, I was needed by others to help them be successful, and if my life was failing in any way, no-one would notice because I still 'looked' good on the outside. I had a good face for the world. I had simply forgotten who I was, AGAIN, and although my instincts, my soul connection, was igniting and getting stronger, I still had some work to do to find the real me – my inner knowing, my SOUL!

This was now my fourth decade, and this coincides with the fourth stage of Alchemy which is called Conjunction. At this stage of Alchemy, or soul transformation, we should have learned from the first three stages – Calcination, Dissolution and Separation. Remember those stages? Fire, water and smoke(-ing mirrors)!

I should have been paying attention to my soul by now, but my powerful Ego, was taking me down another route. This immense, powerful, and very overactive mind of mine, which I was always trying to prove was so special, was certainly very clever and protective, and 'it' kept telling me to believe in others, believe in all you see around you. I was also shown that when you are intuitive, you are being 'floaty', ungrounded, **not** living in the REAL world.

I am laughing now as I can really see what my parents did to me. They told me 'get a real job', a good, honest, and respectful job with the government, nothing floaty like art school where inspirational and creative people went. Oh GOD, no, get a good grounded life, one with a 'decent' successful person, and life would be amazing. Only it wasn't, and how wrong they were. I should have followed my heart. At this time, I *thought* I **WAS** following my heart, and, for all his issues, Dick was grounded in the real world, material, 'successful' to a degree, popular, and funny. He was so real, just what my parents had always wanted for me, and so different from my first unreliable choice. Can you see what my Ego did? It made my choices fit into my parents' perceptions of the real world, the world THEY wanted for me. Surely now I was being all they wanted with this new grounded and successful relationship.

I look back now on this part of my soul map and wonder where 'I', June, went!

My Ego mind was still the driver on this journey, but my vehicle had failed its MOT (mind over truth). Surely, one would assume, it was now time to get out of neutral, and go full throttle with my vehicle's other gears – my heart and soul. Well, I did always live with hope!

Maybe in essence I felt this, but my mind had other things to conquer. I was going to change Dick, rescue him from himself. He might be on the road to self-destruction but I was his heroine! I would help build his empire, his life, his success. Looking back, I can see *'HE'* became my project! Oh dear me, what was happening? Yes, I was changing, alchemy was happening, but was *this* the way to change my life?

My mind, my Ego chatter said, if he became like me, 'we' would be an awesome couple, we would be immense together; no Ego here then, Junsie? As above so below, we would be one, together, we would want the same things, our goals would be the same, our dreams the same, we would be the 'best' couple, Dick and me... what a team!

Check out Conjunction at the back of the book, it should be about empowerment of our true self, and yet I was still searching for me in others, in their dreams and goals; I was still looking outside of myself.

Chapter 5

Decade: 1990s

It is now 1990, and life is moving forward. Scott will be a teenager this year and Siobhan will be 8; both are amazing children, well behaved, well developed, well adjusted, and extremely popular and loved. They very rarely see their father now, as he has moved on with his life with his new wife. Both children have become used to Dick being in their lives, especially Siobhan; he would appear to have become a new 'Dad' to her!

She adored Dick and this pleased me, and yet, somehow, I felt my son had reservations. Scott did his best to get on with him, but Dick liked to be heard; he liked to be the 'man' of the house and knew best, even although he had never had a child of his own, and did not really know my son at all! Sensitive and caring, Scott did not need another 'father', he just needed a 'father figure' who understood him.

I was enjoying my life when this decade began, my social life was more exciting, and I had many new friends and 'family'. I felt upbeat about all that this 'duo' could create and deliver for our future!

By the end of 1991, Dick and I decided to bring our worlds together. We had triumphed on many things – work, our relationship, money, property, family. We had communicated openly about our money and our legal positions, but as Dick was not officially divorced from his wife, I was a little reluctant to rush into anything. However, he convinced me I had nothing to worry about (or was that my Ego in disguise persuading me? I was beginning not to sense the difference). My head said we were on the same journey, the same map, we were moving in the same direction, and my heart was bursting with joy, love, and good vibes. But where was my soul? Was it even there, or in tune with all the changes?

We finally found the perfect house – a castle in my world; never would I have believed I would live in a house like this! Dick was doing well, so it made sense to me that I must also have been good at **my** part of creating this successful life.

(Soul note: Do you see and understand the stories we sometimes tell ourselves? All Ego. My mind told me to help make him successful and we would all be safe!)

We had bought this beautiful home with my money, as Dick's finances were still 'tied up' in another property. My own little family house did not sell in time, so we bent the rules a little and sold it 'on paper' to my sister, to let us pull the equity from it. That paid all the legal fees, plus it paid our deposit for our new home, and all sorts of other things like furniture, changes to the new house, and much more. I felt empowered and important investing my money to help create our dream life.

Our new family house was finally legally ours, well on paper it was Dicks', but I trusted him; I was in love with him, and this commitment was a huge step for him, too. Why would he do anything to harm his new family?

(Soul note: Do you notice the wording here? It is all about Dick! Where am I at this point?)

I was making decisions to please others, making them more powerful but giving my own power away, step by step. Looking back, I wonder which part of me was driving my alchemy train. Was it my heart, because I truly loved this man? Or was it my mind, as it told me to believe in him? My soul was certainly a silent partner.

Dick would profess his love for me and I always believed him, but looking back I do wonder what kind of love it was he felt. My heart loved him, my body missed him, and my soul – oh here it is, my SOUL – could not understand why there were all these issues on so many levels when our life looked so perfect on the outside.

Our personal life seemed to dwindle when he moved in with me. I had become his cook, cleaner, nurturer, friend, confidante, and 'work-mate'; looking back, I felt more like a mother figure than a soul mate. In quiet reflective times, when I tried to make sense of my life with him, I would remind myself how my ex-husband had made me feel on our honeymoon, or when I was pregnant with his children; thoughts of myself, as a woman, felt threatened and my self-esteem dropped to its lowest ever point.

As the nineties moved on, we all settled into 'perfect' family life on the outside (there is that face for the world again). And because I did feel appreciated and respected in his business, and our social life was busy and fun, my mind would tell me that we were lucky, that we had it all. But there were pockets of unease in this perfect life.

I had begun to notice how Dick spoke to my son. Conversations hardly existed between them, and he spoke to Scott always through commands, always criticising him, judging him. For me, being stuck in the middle of the two men I loved, this was becoming quite an issue at home. And I do not 'do' issues! Only ever a PERFECT face for my perfect world.

So I told my son to 'man up' and told Dick at times 'to listen to him' and hoped they would work it out between themselves, but that was not about to happen. My little girl was growing up. She loved Dick, as he was her father in many ways, and he doted on her. She was his little princess, and a bit of her needed to feel loved by a father figure.

From the late 80s and now into the 90s, my children hardly ever heard from their natural father, and in some ways, I was happy about that. So Siobhan relished her relationship with Dick, who loved her like his own. To me, a man who loved a little girl this much, particularly one who was not of his own flesh and blood, **was** a good man. It was a shame my son and Dick just never seemed to get on.

We spent more money on this now beautiful 'show home', and when that project was finished, Dick decided to sell his small apartment in Spain and buy a share in a villa nearby. We were a team in all ways, and as I had been extremely generous with my own money, which was now all tied up in his name, I assumed the new share in this Spanish villa would also be equal. And yes, my name was added to the legal papers. I was overjoyed, although they had written my name on this document as if I was married to him.

As the years rolled by, I began to see just how complicated my life with Dick was. We spent all our time building a future, a business, a social life, a home; we paid for everything together through effort and money. Yet sometimes I questioned what I actually had! He did love me in his own way, but years of feeling unloved had taken its toll on both of us. I was still a passionate woman but my life felt anything but passionate. We were still a young and healthy couple, so what was this all about? Was it about emotional control, or did he indeed love me in that way? It began to prey heavily on my mind and the more he withdrew, the dimmer the spark of passion in my life there was. A cycle was forming and I had no idea how to deal with these issues; I didn't do issues, remember? I simply put the 'face on' again for everyone to see we were perfect. At least I looked good on the outside, but I sure as hell felt horrible, disgusting, and unloved on the inside!

Dick treated me more like an amazing friend and an appreciated 'housewife'. He loved a clean and tidy – and yes, beautiful – home, and I was great at that, after all I had been in training since I was about five. Sometimes all we spoke about was his business, and I felt like a life coach or counsellor, so I began to question this life. Was he really passionately 'in love' with me, or was he just comfortable with me and loved me for what we had as a family? I knew I was fully in love with him.

(Soul note: Again, look at my words fool-y in love with him, but who was I now? where was I in my soul journey and how

much love did I have for myself? I was always exhausted, giving all of me out to everyone else, and I had forgotten about nurturing my own soul, myself!)

I was starting to question my thoughts and feelings about Dick. Some days I did not even like him for the way he spoke to my son, but I still loved him deeply in my heart. This was different to my marriage. If he had been Tom, I would have given up by now. But this battle of minds was all consuming, it took over, he was a challenge and I for one was not losing the battle THIS time. Everything, this time, had to be perfect. Look at what I had invested in so many ways into this family life.

(Soul note: Oh, there goes that head again, keeping me in pain, keeping me safe from the fear of destruction of what my life is at this point. Love should not be about struggle or winning, about investments or safety, or what others think of you. It simply is LOVE – easy, balanced, simple, peaceful, all perfect; LOVE without exceptions or conditions.)

I began to notice a change in his attitude by the mid 90s. We were settled in our beautiful home, business was thriving, we were a 'successful' couple in everyone's eyes, we were blessed with a wealthy lifestyle, happiness, and opportunities. Mum and Dad were getting better, they were behaving and seeking help for alcohol, and my children were absolutely fine… at least, I thought so! Nany was wonderful, as usual, and my sister loved coming to 'play' with us at weekends in our big dream house, sitting at our unique bar playing music. Life simply could not get better. Then BOOM! Yet another bomb went off.

I had noticed Dick was becoming very secretive, quiet, making excuses not to be at home, and working late every night. That 'gut' of mine just KNEW something strange was happening and I was no stranger to odd behaviour, I had been here before. Rather than confront it face on, or simply go inwards and really trust my gut, I began to seek out psychics, mediums, healers, and books of all sorts. I embarked on a journey to find the 'answers' that would help me solve the mysteries of my life. Why, oh why, was I feeling this way again? After all, when I looked in the mirror of my life, we had it 'all' and we were perfect for each other. We were successful, and of course we were in love, plus we had all the material things anyone would ever need, so what was niggling away inside me?

(Soul note: Notice in this decade that my life was all about the material things –, possessions, position, success, how life appeared to be. My heart was lost, completely taken over by my mind/Ego issues. No wonder I was confused, I was running on empty, exhausted and exasperated!)

My son turned 18 on 5th November, 1995 and we were having a birthday party for him in our local community centre with all Scott's friends, and our friends too, as I liked them to see that Dick was a great 'dad' to my kids. I prepared all the food myself for the 80-plus folk coming, and Dick organised a bar and music. Yet I simply knew his heart wasn't in it. I understood that they never got on, these two, but something else did not feel right. I had been here before so I had to trust my instincts this time. For the past few years my mind had been in control of my life. It had taken over the job of my heart, as I was so busy attending to others' needs and trying to sort out everyone's issues and 'stuff'. I had become so bogged down through the fog of their problems that I couldn't see what was actually happening in my own life; but now my mind had taken over the driver's seat on my journey.

Dick told me he needed to leave early the morning after the party – even though it was a Saturday – as he had to go down to a company in England to train for his business. He was never really 'at' the party, because his head was in packing, dressing, and going away the next day.

He left early the next morning by van, and I just knew he was not 'learning' anything for his business over a weekend, so why was there a rush to get down on a Saturday morning? When he came home on the Tuesday, the distance between us became more obvious. I simply knew someone else was involved, I just had no idea who she was or where she lived.

Scott was worried about me. He knew the implications, and had seen clearly what I had refused to see to this point. We all have our faults, and Dick could be selfish at times, but I thought I had everything under control, what else could he want or need. I was surely indispensable for I gave one hundred percent to my work, my home and him. All this time I thought I was in control life, at least my ego told me that, when all I had truly done was given all of myself away; my love, my energy, my power and had never once looked at where I was in all of our journey. I was fearful now, life was out of control, and I felt scared.

I confessed to my son that I was concerned that Dick was possibly having an affair. This young man put aside his own feelings and the way he had been spoken to over the years, and helped me so much by telling me to follow my heart. He said he would always be there for me, no matter what.

(Soul note: Always respect those who love you and who are truthful to you. Love you, Scotty boy!)

When Dick returned from his 'business' trip, I watched him closely and was convinced something was seriously wrong. Weeks later a football match was arranged between our own company and this English company. I was excited, because now I would be seen as his 'wife', and whoever *she* was would realise he was taken! Oh my, how our minds trick us into believing that what we think and feel is how others think and feel!

The big day came, and my sister came to support me and our company 'football' team. She understood my concerns, and even although she loved Dick, she always believed and trusted me. We had been through so much together, and I am grateful to this day that she was there for me then.

On the morning of this football extravaganza, Dick went out early to buy new clothes. He came in bursting with bags of new trendy jumpers, slacks, shoes, and more, and was so excited as he showed off his new gear. It was the most he had spoken in weeks, outside of business!

I was on my hands and knees scrubbing our kitchen floor while he displayed his new gifts to himself. He literally looked down on me as I continued to scrub, and began instructing me to what to pack in his football kit for the rest of the day. I realise now that I really did everything for him at that time; I was more like his mother than his 'wife' or partner.

He told me to make sure his toothbrush was packed in his kit, which I thought was strange – who packs a toothbrush to play a game of football? Then the penny quickly dropped. Whoever 'she' was, she was here with this visiting company, and my gut told me she was the one he had gone to visit the day after my son's 18th birthday.

Even though Scott was also playing in the game, he was asked to make his own way there. Dick set off from our house on foot – bag all packed for him, as per his instructions – and had arranged to meet their bus at the end of our road. He left with a smile on face and his packed football bag in hand, but my petty – yet worried – mind had decided not to pack his requested toothbrush and expensive aftershave.

Scott joined our company football team that day and scored the only goal of the match; I cheered so loudly for him, my heart bursting with pride. I noticed a tall older-looking woman with a 'frail' young man beside her, and wondered who she was. I had nodded a few times but she never responded to me, which was strange. Little did I know this was HER, the other woman! I never saw Dick again that day, not even that night at the party which our two companies threw in a local pub. He preferred to leave me on my own so that he could be with this other woman in the hotel room he had booked for her in another town.

It seemed that he was now *her* knight in shining armour, as I discovered her son had cancer. This seemed to be a pattern he was repeating for this had happened before we lived together, being there for another girl whose mother faced cancer. Now this woman's son was battling the disease and Dick was supporting her through it, maybe I should have been proud of him.

(Soul note: Patterns again. What were these repeating patterns reflecting back to ME? Tom had done the same, he had helped his 'girlfriend' who had heart disease by sending money to her, taking care of her – at the expense of our marriage. This was a similar pattern again, with Dick the caring Knight, coming to the aid of women who were low and going through a hard time! RESCUING OTHERS! I simply could not see that I, too, had been rescuing others all the time. Maybe this was why he repeated this pattern, because I held no challenge for him; I did not need rescuing, I was the rescuer. Maybe these souls made him feel better about himself, boosting his Ego, proving he WAS a great man, after all, or maybe it was just the thrill of the chase, and I was too safe, too strong, and too boring. Maybe this was simply his soul patterns I could not understand, the mirror was reflecting stories back to me and I could not see them. Those smoking mirrors were there, I simply needed to get the lesson.)

He stayed out all night with her, so I locked him out of our home the next day. How dare he think he could just come back and think that was normal behaviour! He sat in the company van in our drive most of that day, then disappeared and booked into another hotel, where he stayed for a few days until all the anger and raw emotions had calmed down.

When he returned home, he promised me that he had learned his lesson and this fling was all over. Like a fool, I took him back. I wanted to believe him, yet I really knew deep down in my heart, my mind was not convinced!

Had he manipulated me again? My head told me it was only a matter of time before this would blow over and he would see what he REALLY had and be very grateful for it.

(Soul note: This sounded like yet another familiar internal dialogue, but it was not a conversation that was taking place with my heart or soul. The mind can be a dangerous tool when working on its own.)

This new friendship continued long distance, and his mobile phone became an appendage to his hand, an extra part of who he was. His phone became a real issue for me, because he could talk to her without me ever knowing. My son became my confidante, as did all my friends who loved me, and I would talk nonstop about him, what he did to hurt me, and what he was turning into. Although they loved me, they would question me as to why I did nothing about the situation; why was I still with him? Looking back now, what was stopping me was FEAR, yet again! Fear was crippling me. I was scared that I was going to lose the love of my life, and my beautiful home, which I had invested everything into.

I was scared to uproot my kids through my bad choices again. What would they think of me? I was scared to fall out with his family, if I made choices against him. I'd lose my car and – worse – my job, and the friends we had together, everything I had come to enjoy through all our hard work. Why should I lose all that when I had done nothing wrong to this man? I was honest, faithful, hard-working, loyal, forgiving and loving. What was there not to like in this life – he had it all, and I would go all out to remind him of that.

(Soul note: Where was my heart and soul guiding me in all this? Simple answer, I could not hear them for the deafening voice of my thoughts, my mind with all its analysing, inner dialogue, internal chatter. I was slowly allowing my fears to paralyse me into NEVER acting upon my intuition, my heart and soul. I had a lot to learn!)

Scott had tried to warn me and I should have listened to my son. He saw Dick through very different eyes to Siobhan and me, and he had overheard Dick boasting about this woman to someone else. I should have listened, but I avoided the truth. I went to a place of fear, a place where I felt completely trapped within our beautiful surroundings. It was a legal mess and I had nothing on paper, so my mind kept telling me to ride the storm, it would all work out sometime. After all, I was strong, I had survived many a turmoil in life, so I would win this battle if it killed me! And slowly my spirit was indeed dying, my soul losing the will to live, my heart literally broken, I became a slave to my thoughts, I simply could not see that it was becoming my fault.

I felt my life spiralling out of control through sadness, fear, worry, and disillusionment, and took to reading numerous self-help books. This horrible situation had unleashed a new journey of self-discovery, a new pathway into trying to understand, not only my instincts, but my latent ability to tune into people and situations, into healing myself and others, and broadening my 'other worldly' knowledge. In a way, this painful situation's side effect of new knowledge helped me 'heal' my relationship with Dick and I 'forgave' him. Relieved, I moved on from it.

Life eventually returned to 'normal' again and I felt stronger, our relationship seemed better, and that Christmas, Dick proposed; this was all I had ever wanted, and when I pulled a cracker on Christmas morning, a beautiful diamond solitaire ring fell out! My daughter screamed with happiness, but my son withdrew from any celebrations. He was wiser than I gave him credit for.

Siobhan loved Dick with all her heart. She even wanted to change her surname to his as she wanted him to be and feel like her proper dad, because unfortunately her own father had never shown her a huge amount of love or interest in her life so far. We spoke about it as a family, but no matter what Tom had been like with her, I felt he was still her dad and we should leave things as they were.

Scott became distant and seemed to spend more time in his bedroom. I knew it was because Dick was firmly in our lives now and in the future. Scott did not trust him because of what had happened in the past, and they just didn't get on. But it was my life, too, and Scott would have his life to look forward to soon enough. I loved Dick, we were strong now, and at least Siobhan was excited about this new project. We had a wedding to plan!

We made plans to get married in April the following year, and with the celebrations of engagement, Christmas and New Year behind us, I was slightly puzzled at the responses of some family members about our future plans. Little statements here and there played havoc with my mind, undermining the joy of what would be the 'wedding of the decade'.

(Soul note: Even now, after getting what I wanted, I was still doubting my self-worth, doubting who I was, questioning all those little comments from others and allowing them to kill my spirit yet again. Where was my Inner Goddess now?)

We settled into 'engaged' life, and our friends forgot all about the last 'drama' and my never-ending rants about it as we began making exciting wedding plans. I organised the outfits, had them specially made by a designer, and chose 30 guests for a quiet wedding meal; each was to be given a personalised crystal wine glass as a gift, no expense spared. Limousines were organised for the wedding party and my son agreed to walk me down the aisle. The cake was made, the band paid for, and the evening party arranged for over 100 friends and family.

I took control again and had special invitations made for our 'heart' themed wedding, yet I noticed that the excitement seemed to be only coming from me! As time went on, I noticed Dick becoming subdued when I spoke of the wedding plans, and eventually I almost became scared of mentioning anything wedding related to him. This was not how I had expected it to be; weddings were special, important turning points in life, yet this build-up was becoming difficult to even discuss. Dick became secretive, quiet, and strange, and I had seen these signs twice before. It was so scary to watch, but now blatantly obvious to me that someone else was on his mind; I simply had to find out who she was.

I thought over what had been happening these past few weeks, and the only thing we had done out of the ordinary was to place an advert in the paper for more staff. Piecing it together, I realised that it had been since then that Dick had changed, working late every night. In fairness, we were busy, but not to that extent. One evening I stayed late with him, making the excuse that I was catching up on overdue paperwork, but he became agitated and kept insisting that I should go home. At about 8pm, the office phone rang. Our business was closed, so who could be calling so late?

I answered the phone and he turned white with fear as a woman's voice asked to speak to him. She coldly gave her name and my body began to shake; something deep within me seemed to know who this was. I felt sick in my stomach as I handed the phone over to him, and I knew this was not good. He took the call from this woman in front of me and spoke in one word, coded answers, and I realised I should be very worried about this situation.

It was January, only 3 months before our wedding, and she was well and truly involved in his life. I began to see his patterns return: the secrecy; his mobile phone now security-coded so I could not get into it; working late most nights; and the silence between us was deafening. I tried talking to him but he would just tell me I was worrying over nothing, and there was nothing going on. But his face told another story, and his demeanour belonged to a condemned man!

When the wedding was only weeks away, I was beside myself with fear. The anxiety was mixed with confusion, and disappointment that this special exciting time was being marred by his lack of love, honesty, respect and enthusiasm. I had felt these same feelings during my pregnancies too; celebrations marred by sadness. I was embarrassed with his behaviour, and dumfounded. Friends were also aware of what he was doing to me, and yet again I was being shown that I was simply not good enough. Even though he went through the motions daily and continued to make arrangements for our wedding, my heart was already broken. The day he went for his wedding suit fitting, he was like a man waiting for death to arrive. And I knew that was what he had done before; I recalled his words from years before that he had married his first wife because he felt obliged to go through with the wedding.

It emerged that this woman who had called him at work was a former girlfriend. I was told she had come between him and his first wife too. His family knew her and had liked her, and now, I felt I was on the outside of my entire life looking in at someone else's journey.

Three weeks before the wedding, after the invitations had been sent to all our family and friends, I sat in our office facing him when the phone rang. I could see the call was being made from an unknown payphone, which I had come to realise was her. I asked him to take the call to enable me to see how he would deal with it knowing I was right there, and he reacted with one-word replies and coded language, finishing off with a 'speak later'. Those words were the last thing I remembered when BOOM! Another of those now massive bombs went off inside my head, and I simply lost it; I had finally been pushed to my limit.

I asked him outright who he wanted – her or me. There could be no more hiding from this now, but all he could say was that he did not know what the future held for us! He did not have the courage to give me a straight answer, and so, as usual, I made the choice for him. I called my dad first to tell him the wedding was off, because Dick had another woman. I then called every guest personally and told them why I had cancelled the wedding at short notice, that Dick was unsure of what the future held for us.

I felt strong, empowered by the truth now. I simply could not allow myself to stand in church and take vows with a man who was 'unsure' about his future with me, or what his feelings were. I would not marry this man when he obviously felt he 'had to' go through with *our* wedding, just like before. I was doing for him what he should have done for himself. Even now, a broken heart, I was rescuing him! Drama and reaction never make for good decision-making. The head took over yet again, where in the stillness and refuge of my heart lay only love but I just could not hear or feel it!

My son was disgusted with him, my daughter was broken-hearted, and I was embarrassed, confused, hurt and angry. When I went to see his family to tell them personally, they seemed to be expecting it. That spoke volumes to me.

The next few weeks were so tense, and there was no communication; I moved into a spare room and we lived separately under one roof. He kept telling me he loved me, that he was sorry, that it was all his fault and he had wanted the wedding to go ahead. But his words meant nothing to me. He had already ruined our special day and our future. Trust was totally shattered now, and I really felt dead inside.

He laughingly still went on his 'stag' holiday – a golfing week with all his pals – as if nothing had happened, but this time-out gave me a chance to think about myself. I was so unhappy and worried. After he came home, it was as if he simply just got on with life again, oblivious to all the pain he had created. Yet I was as low as I could get. About a month later, he left to live elsewhere for a few weeks to clear his head. Those few weeks turned into many months.

(Soul note: He had done this before, always retreating in times of great stress or self-imposed trauma, so he too had repeating patterns from his journey in life. These were seriously affecting my own soul, because I was allowing his patterns to affect me, as if I did not have enough of my own programmes to deal with!)

Eventually he came back home to start afresh again. But, believe it or not, the same woman reappeared and this pattern of behaviour continued to be played out for so long that it became almost the 'normal' way of life for me.

(Soul note: His patterns were being constantly replayed through many women he encountered on his path. Maybe it was commitment that seemed to be an issue, or lack of control, but it seemed he was always looking to see if the grass was greener elsewhere. Now, I could hardly see if these spiralling ugly patterns were mine or his, or both, but I do know they were killing my spirit in all ways.)

My soul was so broken, fragmented now, that I had no idea who I was any more. I was reading more and more self-help books on many varied subjects of meta-physics and mysticism, which was one positive outcome from a very dark time. I rang even more psychics, always looking for the answers to my problems outside of me, and hoping that these complete strangers could see into the life I thought I wanted. It was during these dark and turbulent years that my interest in healing, learning Reiki, and searching for ME happened; I wanted inner peace and love from a different source, and began to have amazing insights and experiences once I had opened up to this energy.

This very turbulent decade began with a man I loved and an exciting, positive and abundant future ahead, but by the end it had come full circle. I was ending these horrible 10 years by selling my beloved home – a home I had cherished, spent lots of money on, ploughed all my love and energy into, and where I had created an amazing garden and beautiful rooms, but it was not a happy home.

Scott had left the year before, unable to remain at home any longer. He needed to experience life without all this heartache surrounding him. I missed him terribly, but in going his own way he was happy, renting my old house – his childhood home – with two friends. He had met a lovely girl and seemed very happy.

Siobhan and I left our beautiful home for the last time in December 1999. As I turned the key on what was a beautiful house, with some special memories for all of us, I took cold comfort in remembering it had never been a proper home. She and I were starting adventures anew in a little tenement flat above shops not far from her school.

Dick? Well, he was still trying to sort out his head, his heart, and his life. Looking back over this decade, it was full of endings, beginnings, and lots more endings, and also lots of unfinished business. But I was on a different path now, one of learning all about me, about absorbing all I could on all mystical subjects, broadening my mind, and learning to fall in love with my lost soul once again. The way I looked at life was that all this pain and trauma, these twists and turns, was not for nothing. Something new and better had been created from it – new beginnings and new insights that were now fuelling my empty heart.

I had learned Reiki, and I knew I was good with this energy work and a competent healer. I began to study books on a variety of subjects, and my dormant psychic abilities began to filter into a very different June. Was the phoenix finally beginning to rise from the ashes... at last? Maybe, but this phoenix was certainly changing –a little more slowly than most, but a change was definitely happening.

Now, why not see if I am catching up with my alchemy train. This decade refers to Fermentation. Maybe alcohol was going to be more prominent! However, the true meaning of this stage of alchemy can be found at the back of the book.

Chapter 6

Decade: 2000, A new century begins!

My beautiful daughter has now grown into an amazing young woman, she is glowing and seems happy, and we are now living together in our 'girly pad'. We left our family home in early December 1999, exactly 7 years to the very month we had moved there – alchemical transformation right enough! They do say, whoever *they* are, that life changes every 7 years!

Dick and I decided to be civil to each other after going our separate ways and we tried to remain friends for Siobhan's sake, because she loved him like a father. For that reason, I agreed he could come and visit us on Hogmanay 1999 to bring in not only a new year, but a new century with us, as a family!

Dick had many sides to his personality, but in my heart I always saw that caring, funny, loving, generous side of him – and that was my downfall.

He began to visit us regularly, which was nice on one hand but not good for me on the other. I found it very confusing, because we were now separated, living in different houses, and yet he kept saying how sorry he was and asking if we could try again. I knew I still had 'feelings' for him somewhere deep in my big, open heart, but I was wary. I enjoyed my own space with Siobhan these days, our pyjama days watching cartoons, being me, having complete control over the TV remote, eating what I wanted and when I wanted it, and especially reading all my amazing New Age books. Being on my own, without constantly looking over my shoulder or fogging up my mind with thoughts of him and what he was doing, I began to open up more to spirit. I learned ways to improve my connection through lovely souls like Collette Brown , an amazing woman, who ran the Psychic Centre in Hamilton at the time. I lived for those Friday nights, and no-one knows how much those evenings gave me, as I began to believe in myself again. (Thank you, lovely lady, from my soul to yours! You gave me an opportunity to have faith in myself again.)

A new me grew from all that had happened in those dark days. I was like a mushroom, sprouting from all the shizzle of my life! My trust had been shattered with all those booming bombs that kept going off in my world, and our new, simple but peaceful abode, I wanted to rest awhile, recuperate and assimilate. But Dick was insistent.

A month later, just as life seemed to settle, another bomb went off. I was just beginning to feel that a better relationship had evolved from the last war. Dick told me everything was going to be different, and we could create a new life together. He had already got into my heart and my head again, then he dropped the bombshell – he had just bought another house... for himself!

I crumbled, because there was no way I could live with the threat of living that way again. I had ploughed precariously through our last years as a couple, trying to hold myself together through fear of many things and mistrust, all the while still running his company. If I am honest now with myself, fear had made me stay longer in the relationship; I was scared that I had too much to lose. I had put a brave face on for all the world, to show I could cope with anything, I was strong, and I was resilient.

(Soul note: There is that old pattern again. As long as your outward appearance in life shows no dirt, as long as you look strong and resilient, then you ARE! But, really, how were you, June? Shattered, fragmented, tired, disillusioned, angry, frustrated, scared, disappointed? Does this sound like a happy soul?)

It is only in looking back now that I can see how Dick knew my weaknesses. I so wanted to believe him; my heart loved the man who could be loving, decent and supportive. So when that part of him promised me that nothing like before would ever happen again, I wanted to believe him. The battle was within me – my head told me I was an intelligent person, clever, brave and forgiving. So the stirrings in my heart convinced me to move my personal belongings into Dick's house only four months later, and left my girl alone in our flat. As the lease ran till June that year, my head told me I had an escape route should I need it, and that my girl would be safe. I was happy now knowing I could return to live at my own place if I needed space.

But I soon felt settled in this lovely bungalow. I loved that it had beautiful established gardens for me to work on, and adored the fact that this new home had the potential for lots of improvements so we could our own stamp on it. (Can you see a project looming again?) Most of all, I loved the new version of Dick. He was just amazing.

My friends were confused, as was my family, but I felt he had turned a corner; he had obviously learned from his mistakes of the last decade and was now making a huge effort! In June that year, with time running out for my lease on the flat, Dick asked me to move in permanently. He felt it was the perfect way forward for both of us, time to put the past behind us and confidently step forward. I thought he was being romantic, but after discussions about improvements to his home, I began to question the reasons I found myself there. I wanted to believe he loved me and could not live without me, but a huge question mark buried its way into my mind. There was no way at this early stage was I ready to fully invest all of me. Maybe I had learned not to be so trusting.

I had been here before; lack of control for seven years had created a fear anchor in me. I needed to know I could leave if things changed. This time the only investment I wanted was to be with him. He had bought this house and it was his responsibility, so if things did not work out, we were both free to leave! Maybe I HAD listened to inner guidance, after all!

I considered myself to be a generous person, money was not *my* problem. However, I obviously feared it in some way, as unknown to me then, I was putting fear of money firmly in its place. I moved in anyway, and worked hard at yet another new project. Our lives were always held together with projects!

(Soul note: The noun PROJECT means 'something that is contemplated, devised, or planned; a plan or scheme; a large or major undertaking, especially one involving considerable money, personnel, and equipment; a specific task or investigation.' I still didn't get the meaning of this word!)

I finally sold my old family house where my kids had been brought up, and where Scott had been living up to this point. On one hand, I felt relieved that, along with that part of my past, it was now gone. But I made no money from the sale. All that was left over was an endowment policy that I was now no longer paying into; it was just sitting there gathering, oh yes, equity for my future. So what did I do? I cashed it in and received £3000 from it, which I then ploughed into a new business venture with Dick. Yet another project was looming, holding us together in a new way.

Dick wanted to improve this house and the best part of the next year was spent creating yet another beautiful home, garden, and more. I bought lots of new things to adorn this house – his house – and the garden, and used my creative, artistic skills to make a beautiful living space for us, and Siobhan, who had moved in with us, too. She had the front of the house for her own space and privacy, so when her boyfriend visited, they had space to chat, watch films, and enjoy their young lives. Ever hopeful (or stupid), I had hoped we would all get on brilliantly and recover from the civil war of the last decade! Well, that was the plan, but then I began to notice the same old patterns starting again. This time, Dick constantly picked fault with Siobhan's boyfriend in the same way he had picked fault with my son. It made her life very uncomfortable because, unlike our last home, this was definitely his!

The secret calls began again, the mobile phone was left in the car and not brought into the house after work, and he would disappear to visit others on his own and not invite me. Then strange calls started at the office, and my stomach churned. My head was now 10 steps ahead, which was not helped by him working late yet again. There were whispers at work when he was not there, and it was beginning to really upset me. I had been here so many times, and this time around I knew exactly what was happening.

He had lured me back with all the promises of change, worked my socks off both at work and home over the past year, and then, when the projects were all finished and he was possibly bored with me or life, it began all over again. Patterns? These were the ugliest repeating patterns ever!

It was now obvious that he was cheating on me again with another woman, although this was not just any woman. It was the same one who had come and gone throughout the previous decade, ruining our wedding, nearly ruining my life and my health, and now she was back again. I was completely overwhelmed; words cannot express just how shocked I was.

She was back with a vengeance, and the timing was strange, because it came to light after I had invested so much of myself in many ways into this fresh start! What a lovesick fool I had been. What an idiot. I had been free and secure in my own life, but here I was again – only this time it was worse. I would need to leave his home with my belongings in it and find a new home yet again. My body was so tired, my mind was filled with confusion, and my bruised Ego just shouted at me: YOU FOOL!

The arguments, accusations, and silences began all over again, and eventually Siobhan left and got her own place. This man was driving my children away from me and driving me into the ground. After Siobhan left, I remained in this hell, fear yet again paralysing me into submission; experiencing guilt and regret at having made more disastrous decisions; embarrassed that I allowed him to make a fool of me again; scared – no, actually I was terrified – of the reasons he had wanted me back in his life. Did I really know him at all? What was he capable of? I was weak, I was scared, I was unhappy, and totally devastated that I found myself back in this position once more.

I reached outside of me for more psychic readings, and all of them said it would work out, it would be fine, he was a good man. And I BELIEVED them! But that was not what my heart and soul were telling me. They were shouting: 'Run for the hills! We have your back, we will always love you. Get out of this revolving doorway for the last time!'

I was reaching out to analyse *him*, looking at *his* behaviour, but never once stopped to look inside my own heart! It was broken, I was broken, and on top of this, I had to face going to work daily with him, a place where the calls from her, coupled with all the rumours, sniggers and looks of sympathy, added to the pressure of my ever deflated heart. I wanted to prove everyone wrong; I wanted to show people I was a good judge of character and that he was, deep down, a great man, maybe just weak or a troubled soul.

(Soul note: Oh, June, and you thought he was the rescuer! You trusted his words again and now, in all your pain, who were you trying to convince – others or yourself? Whose opinion was more important? Why was my mind still running the show, fear telling me to stay, keeping me trapped in this hell, making me feel small, useless, keeping me 'safe' in this unsafe world. This mind bomb would explode soon enough.)

Going back a little in time, in March 2001 – while I was still living there – something profound happened to me while reaching out to understand him through spiritual readings. I had a soul reading that would change my life in a very different way; it was like no other reading I had ever experienced. It was channelled by a beautiful lady called Emma, who had been trained by a well known author in metaphysical studies, David Cousins, author of *A Handbook for Lightworkers.* And the way she worked felt so right for me. She tuned directly in with my higher self or soul and, with permission, she downloaded information my soul was seeking to understand how to move forward in life. Unlike all the others, this reading was not about impending doom, gloom and boom. It was not about Dick. It was 'soul-fully' about me! It was the day my life began to change, because I resonated with this information in a new way. This taped reading shook the core of my 'world' as I knew it. There was so much in all this information she spoke of that I simply did not understand, but somehow I trusted it. Funny how I seemed to trust the words of others far more than my own words or thoughts!

She spoke of things I had never heard of – the Law of One, the Great White Brotherhood, inner plane work and opening portals. Yet, although it seemed overwhelming and new to me, for some strange reason somewhere deep within me I trusted this information. I simply knew with great clarity that this was important for me, and I had not felt clarity for a long while.

(Soul note: Going back to my childhood, I remembered the feelings of love and trust that came when I saw the cloaked figure when I was only 8 years old. It was that sort of knowing again; I simply KNEW this was right for me! When you listen to your heart, your soul, that inner voice, it sounds like a trusted and loving friend, an inner knowing, and your mind – although an amazing tool – can be the trickster at times. So get to know all parts of you.)

I listened to this channelled information time and time again, and in this dark time of my journey, it gave me immense hope, an inner knowing, strength, and trust in myself again. I realised that I was here for a reason, and that this life with all its stories and dramas was not all of it! I was not here just to rescue and heal Dick, or rescue and heal my mother and father. I also had a soul purpose, a mission all of my own, and one day I would know what that was!

This information Emma had given me spoke of ancient knowledge I was able to download and channel, called Science of the Heart or Medicine of the Heart, and that one day scientists would come into my life and our paths would cross between science and spirituality. This also felt right. I tingled inside every time I listened to the tape, and I tried to find information on this ancient healing she called Science of the Heart but I never could.

Lots of other jigsaw pieces of my massive soul puzzle fell into place around me. Some felt immediate from the reading, but others seemed way out of my reach. Some, on the other hand, I just could not see me doing; I had never heard of them before! However, my soul deeply understood that reading on many levels, and it changed something in me at that point. I began a new journey, one of deeper self-discovery and self-belief. I felt that even although my life was falling apart around me again, other parts were coming together. I had something tangible now, something was going to save me. I never knew at that point that it was my own soul.

Later that month I decided I'd had enough of living like a scared prisoner in this house that would never be looked on as our home. There had been no signs of phone calls for a while, but my gut kept telling me she was out there and still part of his life. It seemed like they were unable to stay apart. On this particular day, I felt I had to start looking for a new place to live, to get that inner peace again, and somewhere I could stop walking on eggshells, scared of my own shadow. I had no way of knowing where, or how, but I was beginning to listen to that inner voice. You know that voice, the one that belongs to your soul.

I was 'guided' to a house leasing company close by, and it turned out that a flat, situated right across from where my daughter lived, had just come up for lease that very day. How strange! I could get the keys immediately if I wanted, but my head kept telling me I needed another reason to leave. I had to justify this move to my head, as if what was happening around me was not enough. I needed a last push to leave him, my mind taking charge of my inner dialogue, analysing again, looking for ways to keep me safe, to keep me trapped. Did I really want to leave, after all of the hard work I had put into his house? How powerful our mind chatter becomes when we are not in balance with our heart and soul!

Although I knew my heart was right this time, I still needed proof that my instinct was right. I clearly still did not trust myself or my own judgement any more! After viewing this potential flat, I returned to work, a broken woman, to find him laughing and joking with staff as if nothing was wrong in his life, he had not a care in the world. Who was putting a face on the world now? I realised at that point that I hardly recognised this stranger as the man who had pleaded with me to come back into his life. My inner voice told me to go out onto the factory floor, and as I walked about the large machinery and benches, chatting to the workers, I noticed a new mobile phone being charged up. No-one seemed to know who it belonged to.

I asked one of the engineers about it, he told me that it belonged to Dick and that he kept it there all the time. Right away I got it: I was being made to look the idiot, the troublemaker, the drama queen, the one with the severe issues of mistrust for he was answering his mobile in front of me - I was simply paranoid. But here was a second phone; why? Who needs two phones?

I made an excuse to leave work for an hour, went back to the leasing company, paid two months' rent and got the keys of this flat. Now I simply had to find a way of getting out of the house with all my belongings.

I got home, my stomach now churning. I felt sick, my mind was racing, and yet I knew I was right! I made a call to a mutual friend with all my concerns, and told him what had transpired and that I wanted to leave, and leave with all my things. My good friend simply stated one sentence that changed my fear into power: 'Possession, June, is 9/10ths of the law!' Within minutes I was searching for a removal firm who could take me and my belongings to my own little haven, near my beloved girl, as soon as possible.

The soul – your soul – when in power, is simply amazing. As I phoned a local removal company to enquire about getting me out of this house, they told me that just minutes before they had received a cancellation for the very next morning. How strange, you may think. But, trust me, when you work from your heart, when you allow your soul to guide you and drive your vehicle, amazing things happen quickly and the heart and soul conspire for your perfect outcome. I did not hesitate, because it seemed that when I listened to my soul's guidance, things moved faster than the speed of light!!

The move was fast and furious. The next morning I played 'sick'; in some way I was not lying, for I was truly sick – sick, too, of this life! Within a few hours of Dick leaving for work, I was gone, along with everything I had paid for in my life with him. I had the receipts to prove it and, as my friend said, possession was the law! He had his stunning new home, I had my only belongings.

He never knew I had gone until he returned from work that day. Part of me realised I had offered him the same lesson he had played out to his first wife. He had left her with no explanation, packing up and leaving without warning. I wondered if his heart and soul ever got that!

Only Siobhan knew where I lived now, and within an hour of moving in, I had my pictures up, curtains up, and champagne opened. I have to thank a good friend of mine at that time for helping me, and my cousin who was there to protect me in case Dick came to try and stop me. Even although I nearly fainted outside my new abode as the adrenalin stopped pumping through my veins, I knew I was safe. I could finally relax as I was free again, and I could begin the healing recovery of my mind, body, and soul.

Having Siobhan so close to me was amazing again, and life was peaceful. I had got into the habit of parking my car away from my flat so that no-one would know where I lived. My mobile phone was being bombarded with messages of how sorry he was, to talk, promises that we could 'fix things'. Ring any alarm bells?

All was peace and quiet until one particular night a few weeks later. I knew Dick had been out looking in our area because he knew where Siobhan lived, but this night he had seen my car in front of my own flat. I remember saying to her that I had a feeling we were being watched then… BOOM. My door was battered in this 'secured entry' flat. I knew it was Dick and that he had found me. My heart was pounding and I shook from head to toe. Why should I be so scared? What had happened to that young warrior?

As Siobhan and I quietly moved in the darkness from the kitchen to look out the window, two piercing eyes were staring at us through my letterbox! I can laugh at this now, but at the time I was traumatised. Dick had been drinking and was shouting at me to open the door. I had no intention of letting him in, so I called my son and he came to my rescue like my own knight in shining armour, getting Dick out of the building and safely into a taxi and he took him home. No matter what his feelings were about this man, my son took the lead that night, and showed what he was made of. He was the adult now.

Dick would sit outside my flat phoning me in the early hours of the morning. He wanted answers as to why I had left him the way I did, which is quite funny because I was the one who **really** wanted answers. I agreed to meet him in a car park for ten minutes, because I did not want him getting back into my soul. I was not the same quiet, forgiving woman that had lived with him before. I wanted to know why he had allowed this woman into our lives yet again. Why had he bought a second phone ? Why did he always want me back, then completely destroy our relationship and lives every time?

He told me they had history together, he did not want me involved with her and that he did not love her but felt an obligation to help her.

(Soul note: His patterns resurfaced again, the need to rescue others at any cost to himself and to 'us'.)

Again, I let him in, believing now that I understood his situation more. It was possibly his old fears, so I forgave him yet again.

By now, even *you* could write the script of my life! And hopefully now you can see how easily we can destroy our lives, why we repeat patterns, beliefs, habits, and programmes, why and how our mind creates situations, fear, limiting beliefs about ourselves, our soul, and how we may live for or are addicted to the drama, the story, the illusion. But *none* of this is real.

The part of all of us that truly *is* real, is our amazing soul. But how often do you truly connect and listen to this true authentic part of you? I did occasionally, and when I did, I saw that things happened fast. When I truly listened to my heart and soul… BOOM, life fell into place with immediate and perfect effect! I had witnessed and experienced this with my own eyes, and felt it deep in my heart. How else could I have secured a flat one day, and be living in it less than 24 hours later?

Sometimes, however, the mind kicks in and tells us another 'truth', and when we separate our mind from our soul, we can create and live a very different outcome. Our heart always says to follow your soul, as it WILL keep you safe. And when our beautiful, creative, intelligent minds are in balance with our heart and our soul, magic simply happens!

I could go into many of the 'dramas' of the next few years, where Dick kept repeating his patterns, allowing his mind to rule his path and his head to rule his heart, but what would be the point? I am sure you can see it for yourself. I had issues with trust, rejection, self-belief, and so much more. And he had his own issues. We were simply not a match made in Heaven, and although I thought it was my heart that allowed me to keep taking this man back, I realise now that it was my head, my addictions, my patterns.

Please don't think that my heart was void of feelings. I **knew** I had feelings for him, but I could not get out of my stories long enough to actually feel what these feelings were. Our lives came and went until the death of my beautiful Nany in 2002.

He was there for me in many ways, supportive and kind. He helped our family, too, and it was beautiful to see that side of Dick. He could be so caring and loving in times of need, but I could see that his patterns of rescuing damsels in distress was feeding his Ego. The insane habit now of coming and going, moving from house to house, power struggles, all became tiring. And I decided a year after my Nany had passed on that I needed a break from everyone and everything.

It was September 2003. Alone, in the sultry heat of our villa in Spain, I spoke to my beautiful Nany as if she was sitting right beside me, listening intently to me as she always had all my life, non-judgemental, just listening with her open heart. I asked her for a sign – again, my need to know from outside of me – that she was indeed there. And as I type this, I can feel tears well up, because just as I asked for this sign from her, I saw the beautiful flowers I had bought for her first anniversary of going home to God, move on the coffee table. Part of me began analysing this: was it her? Who was it? Could we have a Spanish ghost? Maybe it was the heat getting to me. Questions and thoughts filtered in and out of my mind, forgetting what I had just witnessed was a true miracle of her presence! She was probably saying, 'Thank you for the flowers and I am here with you, listening as always!'

I went outside and lay down in the warm sunshine and thought about my life with her, felt her love around me, and distinctly heard her speak to me. The words were out of the blue, not attached to my thoughts at all, and felt so right that I immediately understood the message. I heard her say, 'When you get home, open a shop and help others listen to their hearts.'

I had been thinking about making a move from Dick's business, because it was difficult working with and for a man who I felt had disrespected me most of our lives, and working with him constantly brought painful memories of all that had happened. I had told my daughter that on my return from this holiday I was going to leave my job. That daily tie to him through work was now unbearable and it was time to be my own woman.

When I got back, I tried to contact him through his mobile and left many messages on his voicemail to get in touch immediately. Our latest joint home, which was now up for sale, was another one that he had wanted but hardly lived in. I have kept details to the minimum here, because it had been my last big mistake .

It had been a very painful last experience, plagued by all sorts of horrors but now a potential buyer wanted to come and see it immediately. As Dick refused to answer any of my relentless calls about our house, I finally relented and called someone close who may know where he was. I was told that he was away for a break in Edinburgh with a friend.

This time I laughed. I was no longer upset, and it just convinced me that I was doing the right thing, because nothing would ever change. I put all the clothes he had left at our house in bin bags and left them at his factory, then I let his friend know that he should collect them when he returned. But I discovered they were at hospital with him, as he had been attacked during his weekend away. My gut had one of those feelings again, but this was his business and his stuff. I did not care anymore and he could simply get on with it.

That week, I took my letter of resignation to him and was shocked when I saw the state of his face. He would not tell me who did it, just said it was a long story and that one day he would explain. I knew he never would and it really did not matter because I was moving on – at last!

I quit my job – one I had put so much work and energy into since the late 80s – and I was finally free; we both were and the relief was amazing. I was a little wobbly about the fact that I had no income, but I held onto those words I had heard in Spain and believed that I was one day going to open my very own Mind, Body Spirit shop. I did not know how quickly that would happen, but when you live life directly through your soul, and work and think with your heart, amazing synchronicities happen.

That very day, after handing in my resignation, I took a different route home. As I passed a group of small shops, I noticed one had a 'TO LET' sign in the window. I stopped the car and called the number to ask what information they required from me for the lease. I never even asked how much it would cost! Within 4 days of trusting my gut – my soul, where life and decisions seemed to flow fearlessly – I had the keys of that shop and I opened my business the following month.

(Soul note: This is when you know it is your SOUL is fully in charge! This had happened before, many times, and I was now understanding that when you drop fear to live and think from the heart, your soul conspires with the Universe, and life flows, moves you forward, supports you, and blesses you with opportunity!)

I opened the doors of my shop in November 2003 – a magical and mystical haven called Inspirations. I decorated it in lilacs and purples, as these were Nany's favourite colours and I wanted to honour her. As with all of my life, I knew it was her who had guided me that day in Spain, and to this very point of my journey. When I stood inside this very special place, I knew it was her unconditional heart and my brave soul that had led me now to new beginnings.

Siobhan and I sourced everything, from crystals, angels, oracle cards, books, fairies, wizards, Buddha's, singing bowls – you name it, there was space for it. I believe that we are all learning and journeying in different ways and through various beliefs, but all go back to the same place, to the same soul home. So I knew in my heart I had to bring all walks of life into this little Heaven on Earth. I became known locally as the angel lady, the crystal lady, the witchy lady, or that I owned the fairy shop or the crystal shop. People seemed to describe Inspirations in their own way, the way their journey was heading or what interested them.

I set up a local group in early 2004 called Shambhalla, which ran every two weeks. The idea was that this coming together of souls would help everyone, and we would grow, heal, learn all different types of paths in life and share our beliefs and knowledge. I invited speakers from all walks of life and asked them to spread their light and knowledge, and offered a platform for them to grow, too.

Dick came and went from my life, but I chose now never to live with him. We kept in touch for Siobhan's sake and when he was in good form, he was good company, but I had simply knew when to call it a day. He held onto life with us, inviting himself at Christmas or New Year, or birthdays, and this suited him on many levels. He still liked being part of our lives on one level, but we were happier just being friends for Siobhan.

On a cold December night years later, I made it easy for all of us, and I ended the connection completely. We still had villa in Spain and continued to share its costs and upkeep, but it was only through this that we ever spoke again.

My life had changed dramatically thanks to my lovely wee shop, and I was now offering soul readings, similar to the one I had received from Emma in 2001. I was also studying all sorts of therapies and teaching some. Colour therapy was a huge learning curve and the two souls who taught this unique and powerful way to heal – Melissie Jolly and Moira Bush – taught me so very much. I loved working with colour, as the insights were intense and immense. It was while on a course for Colour Mirrors in 2004 that I met an amazing young man who became a great friend, Kyle Gray, known as the Angel Whisperer. Kyle and I struck up a great friendship and he came along to many workshops, conferences and groups that I ran in those days. He was, and is, a truly loving and highly intuitive angel himself, a guiding light for our times. And I look back with great fondness of those early days when he would come along on a Saturday to offer readings from my shop.

Inspirations had been a good name for my shop, because I wanted to inspire everyone who walked through its bright purple door! Looking back, the name was truly meant to be, as before I opened the shop I had a shiny purple and silver sign made for above the window. On the day the sign was to be fitted, my daughter was busy organising shelves for me and went out to check the progress of this new sign. She came running in, her face panicky, and questioned why I'd had this horrible new sign made in black and white. I reminded her it was bright purple, so she must be mistaken. She dragged me out to the front of the shop and I could see they had stripped off all the old signs down to the original sign, which looked like it came from the 50s. As fate would have it, this shop had been originally called Inspirations. So I took it to be another 'sign' that I was in the right shop, doing the right thing, and that everything was going to be right from now on!

Life seemed so much better now. I was living it in my own way; my son was married and enjoying being a husband to his lovely wife Debbie; and my daughter was studying Pharmacology at university after taking a year out. She could turn her hand to many things and was so like her mum in many ways, as nothing seemed to phase her. She was at university studying hard, had bought a flat with her partner, had a part-time job to pay her way, and was looking after her new pup, Nicco. She was a chip off my old block; she tackled anything and everything!

Every now and then I would listen to my special Emma soul tape from 2001 and pick up on certain parts again, sometimes as if discovering the information for the first time. However the one part that kept evading me was that I would be teaching a new way of healing called 'Science of the Heart'. I often wondered about this and where, oh where, were these scientists who were going to miraculously enter my life?

I was in no way a scientist, I was very right-brained, not a very logical being. Just look at all my crazy decisions! My two children had chosen fields of science at university – Scott had chosen Applied Chemistry and Siobhan, although she was originally going to study engineering, had decided on Pharmacology.

It was because of her chosen dissertation subject on heart disease that things began to shift again, and more of those soul jigsaw pieces fell into place. She had decided to submit her dissertation on a topic that normally Pharmacology students should avoid! The subject matter was all about using a natural substance called EDTA to assist in fighting heart disease instead of chemical drugs. Her professor had agreed she could do this, even although she may have created a low pass mark for herself, because she was pressing many buttons in this field of alternative science! But this work she was doing led to a meeting of souls again.

My good friend, Stan Giles, invited myself and Siobhan to a talk at his home, given by a young man I had never heard of. His name was David Hamilton, and instantly I warmed to his funny, down-to-earth approach to science. I discovered he had been a scientist but had left this field to write about the placebo effects of the mind on the body. And I have to say, I liked what I heard!

He was generous of his time and helped Siobhan source material for her thesis, and encouraged her to follow her heart on this. As she followed her heart, she saw all the signs she had been guided by and followed them. By working this way, it led to an amazing piece of work. She could have failed her in her degree, but she did not give into fear and instead her work won her first prize from the Pharmacological Society of Great Britain.

I was delighted for her. But she was upset that she did not get a first class honours with her work. She got honours with distinction and, in her mind, this was simply not good enough for her!

(Soul note: Oh dear, her own patterns were forming about being 'not good enough'. This may have stemmed from lack of contact with her father, with some of my own genetic patterns thrown in for good measure!)

As time went by, David and I became good pals and we had great fun in that wee shop, discussing many topics. He looked forward to his coffee and cake, and I loved his insights into how the mind worked. David was teaching me that the mind WAS a powerful tool, one not to be feared, and that it was the mind chatter, the Ego, that held us captive. He had been writing a book called

It's the Thought that Counts, and I remember offering him an impromptu 'reading' in the shop one day and telling him to hold onto his dream. I said he'd be published by Hay House, and would speak on stage with many of their great authors.

By that point, his book had already been rejected by a few and he decided to self publish it and work out in the field, spreading the word and wisdom he so genuinely owned. It was so right for him to do this. His earthy, funny, and clever insights got the attention of Hay House, who decided to publish his book after all – and look what happened. The rest is history, as they say. It is another example of how, when our soul is in charge and we work from our heart, our mind becomes clear, focused and powerful and can drive all parts of us forward in a balanced, perfect manner.

During my Inspirations years, I began teaching Reiki, colour therapy and I offered therapy sessions in my shop. I also organised the Shambhalla spiritual meetings, and could see that other modalities were needed to be taught so began teaching meditation, psychic development, and offering soul 'coaching'. Life was busy, and yet I was not making ends meet because I had this nature, or pattern, of always wanting to please others.

(Soul note: From early childhood, I had wanted to please my parents, please my teachers, my friends, then please my partners, my kids, and now I was acting this pattern out in my work! When was I going to learn to simply please myself?)

From October 2003 until the summer of 2004 my son came and went from my shop a lot. He had given us the news that he was about to be a father, and Debbie was expecting my first grandchild in mid-September. By April of that year, he was visiting on his own, a lot of the time to talk to me and moan a little about life. I tried to explain that when women are pregnant, their hormones are all over the place, and that he should be gentle with this, and that life would settle down again.

Then that BOOM happened and another unexpected bomb went off. He decided he needed space from his wife, and he felt it was better if he left to straighten out his head.

(Soul note: Wonder if patterns come from only genetic lines, or could the behaviour of all of his elders as he grew up have affected him?)

Siobhan offered him a spare bed at hers –I was already living with her, so now she had all of us there. As I would get up for work, Scott would crawl into my bed when he came off nightshift then sleep all day while we worked. I began to notice signs that something was not right, and I felt his attitude had become strange. This normally loving, kind, sensitive and caring young man was reminding me of his dad!

*(Soul note: Well, what did **you** expect? **You** followed your parents' patterns; he was simply following his!)*

I questioned Scott as to the reason he had needed space, especially with a longed-for baby on its way, as this separation had been so fast, and seemed to have come out of the blue. He spoke about things not feeling right, but none of that made sense to me. I was told that there was someone else involved but I simply refused to believe that for he had always promised me he would never treat a woman the way I had been treated. Gossip can be a destructive energy, however, these dusty bombs had not entirely been disabled and it would seem history was indeed repeating itself!

(Soul note: WOW, how patterns really DO repeat in families. This is exactly what had happened to me when I was pregnant with Siobhan; Scott was repeating his father's patterns. Although the heart and soul may not wish to wreak havoc in this way, our personalities can – look at the history of my own life. Scott had witnessed many repeated programmes from all around him, so why did I expect it would not affect him?)

The day he spoke to me openly about his life choices was nearly the last day we spoke. I was angry for I thought he was ruining his life, and all involved in this heartbreaking situation. I was hurt, frustrated, confused for I could not believe it. There was a part of me still hurting, for this situation was like looking into a mirror of my own past when I was pregnant with Siobhan.

Scott left Siobhan's home weeks later and found himself a place to live, while we all tried to pick up the pieces of this bomb. He never understood that I took 'his wife's side', however, to me, there were no sides; there was just devastation, confusion and hurt, and out of this mess a little baby whom we all had to love. I had told him and Debbie years before they got married that they would have a child and it would be born in an October. Their baby was due on the same date that Siobhan had been meant to be born – as coincidences would have it again

– and as the weeks rolled on, Debbie, with her dignity intact and her non-judgemental ways, was a lesson in life to all of us.

She gave birth with her family by her side on the 4th October, 2 weeks after the baby's due date. My first grand-daughter entered our world – a beautiful little girl who shines so brightly with love, even today. If there were to be sides, then I was on the side of this beautiful, innocent little girl, who is surrounded by unconditional love from ALL her family, and I am just sad that my son is not part of that journey or healing.

Although he no longer speaks to me, I still love my son. We are all very different souls now to we were then, and everyone involved has moved on. I have learned to let go of my past, to release and heal it all, and I would love if my son did the same. He is a free spirit, and I don't own his soul, I would just hope for his sake that he has found peace with it all.

(Soul note: we are not here to live our lives as our fathers or our mothers, we are unique souls here to experience and learn through our own hearts, our free will. Yes, our mind may have been programmed by some of our genetic patterns that were used before. However, we can choose to follow what we know to be true in our heart, or we can blame others for our choices or behaviours. They are all stories our Ego may tell us, as it tries to make sense of life. None of them are important; all that is important is what is in your heart, and how your soul leads the way through forgiveness, grace, and love! Love you, Scott, with all my heart and soul.)

By the end of summer 2007, I reflected back over the years of this decade so far, its highs and lows. I had become a Nana, but lost my son. I had worked tirelessly with my parents for years as they battled with their alcohol abuse and addiction, only to lose my dad to this very drug in 2006. Alcohol abuse had been the reason my mum had a massive stroke years earlier, and was now wheelchair-bound and living in a care home. I had gone back to and fro from my ex-partner so many times that I had lost count. I had also moved home so many times that I sometimes felt I should never unpack those 'boxes' or furniture ever again.

I was constantly shoring up my shop through credit cards and putting my life savings into keeping it buoyant. As my business life mirrored my personal life, I always wanted to please every soul who walked in that door and provide them with whatever it was they were searching for, even when my shop stock was sitting at £60,000 and I had no money to pay my other bills! I had also put on weight during those years, and I know this was how I fed my soul – protective layering from all the hurt and issues I had been dealing with.

I never wanted to hurt again, so if I was fat, no-one would love me or be attracted to me, and at least I would never experience this traumatic pain ever again. Those years felt as if I was spinning plates – I would just have one part healed, sorted, and balanced, when two more fell down. I knew a change was coming, I just did not know what that change was.

During my time in this shop I had met some amazing people, and this experience had allowed me not only to work with them, but to teach them, learn with them, laugh with them, cry with them, and counsel them, as they did me. I met many of my friends through this shop, especially my soul friends Gordon and Ben, who were – and still are – very intuitive and in tune with me. I trusted them so much, and I loved having them as close friends. Still do!

I decided to speak candidly to them one day in my little haven, where both of them helped out from time to time. I explained that I felt guided to sell up, as money – or lack of it – was making me look at my life, my patterns and habits to please others, sometimes before my own needs. The rescuer in me was tired now, and I was constantly giving out and not always receiving. There were my issues and fears with money, the need to put a face on for the whole world, even when I was worried sick inside.

I was tired, and my body, mind and soul needed a break from all this. I asked them to help me with an open day, for I had spoken to God and He told me to 'look for the signs'. I so loved when I got those signs! God only knows, I had missed many more than I ever saw. I advertised an open day for October that year and asked the Universe for a gloriously warm sunny day, which are far and few between in Scottish summers, never mind nearly winter. I also asked for it to be exceptionally busy. If this happened, my soul would know it was time for me to move on. Strange, you may be thinking but in the past, my controlling mind would have told me it was worth holding onto to, but this was to be my sign for letting it go into the hands of another wonderful soul.

The open day came, and the sun was indeed shining; it was so hot that we found chairs and put them outside on the pavement for tea, coffee, and soft drinks to be served to the throngs of souls who came – sometimes 5 deep at my counter! The shop took in more on that one day than I had made in weeks, and yet I knew God was talking to me. My sign was clear, and so I put Inspirations up for sale. Now I was listening to my heart and not my Ego!

By January 2008, my shop was in the safe hands of a lovely soul, Dawnne, who took it over. With my daughter now living in the Middle East, I began to work from her home, which I was now caretaking for her

Her life was certainly following patterns of mine, like the need to please others before herself. She had given up many personal opportunities – one being a place with the British Heart Foundation to study as a doctor, as a result of her amazing thesis. She also had given up a career in the police, to follow her heart, and her partner out to Dubai, for this was his soul journey. My son was also living out there, alongside his father, who had found him work in Abu Dhabi. That was my story twenty years earlier, and where many issues began. We can only guide our children and hope they learn from our past.

Working from home was difficult, and I was hardly covering my rent, my overheads or my credit cards. I loved teaching and mentoring, but nothing was soothing my troubled soul. I remember waiting for Reiki students one day in February, and stood at the door of my flat, watching the rain batter off the ground, my senses smelling its fragrance as it cleansed the garden below. I began to feel a little unsteady on my feet, and a strange numbness took over the left side of my body as my leg began to simply not follow what my brain was telling it to do.

Having seen my mother suffer I stroke, I knew to check in the mirror. I sensed my face was slightly drooped on the left side, and I remember that I seemed to drag my leg, and my arm simply hung. Something in me remembered my mother being told about climbing stairs, so I tried to climb with the support of the 'strange' leg, and fell!

Of course, my sometimes flighty right-sided brain was telling me I was 'ungrounded'; maybe I was having one of my 'out of body' experiences. My mind tried to make sense of this situation every way other than that I might be having a stroke! When the girls arrived, I told them the workshop would start late because I needed to pop out to the doctors to get checked as I thought I may have taken a mini stroke!!

Their poor faces were a picture, sitting on my couch with a cuppa and wanting to leave and do this another day. But all my old patterns rose to the surface – the one about not letting anyone down took over; the other about putting a face on for everyone, even this slightly wonky one; and of course, my people pleasing one. If I am being honest, there was even the fear of money one, as I desperately needed to be paid. I was going to be fine, I had to be, and this workshop *would* go ahead.

I walked the few minutes to the surgery and, after some tests, my doctor explained that I had indeed had a TIA or mini stroke and that my blood pressure was simply through the roof.

(Soul note: That pressure was there always, the pressure to help everyone, the pressure to love everyone, the pressure to live,

the pressure of money, of failure, or fear, now it was high blood pressure. I should have seen THIS sign! According to Louise L Hay, high blood pressure is about unresolved and long-standing emotional problems, and stroke is connected to resistance and rejection of life – rather die than change. My body was trying to tell me what I needed to change in my mind, my heart, and my life.)

Next day at the Stroke Clinic at our local hospital, they confirmed I had suffered a mini stroke and hoped I was not driving. I was, of course, because I had no-one to look after ME! I was always the one who looked after everyone else. So I drove home and reflected on the day before and how, even after knowing I was not well, I had continued to teach Reiki. My speech had been slightly slurred, but I DID it. But **why** did I do it? I was becoming a danger to myself.

My daughter was beside herself with worry when she heard, and suggested I go out for a holiday to Dubai. After getting the all clear, and an early birthday present from her enabling me to get a flight, I took time out to visit her.

I got through the rest of that year, robbing Peter to pay Paul, and as Christmas approached I looked forward to my girl coming home to stay for a wee while. I had missed her. Once the celebrations were over, Siobhan went back to Dubai, and life was mundanely getting back to normal.

I often thought about my shop, and my life so far; I had never thought it would turn out this way. I carried on with workshops and soul readings, offered private consultations in the little therapy room I had created in Siobhan's flat, and I felt well in many ways. My body was overweight, and it felt heavy like my heart some days. I seemed to cut myself off from my past, preferring my own company and finding it difficult to adjust to life as a single woman. I had no desire to find another partner –looking back, I was scared.

My trust had been blown into smithereens so I very rarely socialised, preferring to be with family or my little granddaughter. She lifted my spirits all the time; she was a Godsend at this time of my life. As March approached, I prepared to face the second anniversary of my dad's death, I missed him greatly.

March had barely arrived when I had a call from my very upset daughter. She had just got word that my ex-husband had dropped dead suddenly in Abu Dhabi, with Scott by his side. Both of them had been at the airport waiting on Scott's girlfriend and his new baby daughter coming for a visit. This shocked me. Tom was only in his fifties, and yet, it had been predicted many years before in the many psychic readings I had undertaken that he would die early in life. I could not take it in, and Siobhan was hurting so badly for a father that she loved on some level, but one who had really never got to know his own child.

My son and my daughter's lives were becoming scarily like their mother and father's lives, and this worried me. But all I cared about was my little girl who was thrown into turmoil in the Middle East, with only her brother to show her love and compassion now.

Her partner at that time drove her on the hour-long journey to meet Scott, who was in a state of despair I am told. He had witnessed his father drop dead at his feet and tried to revive him, and my heart was aching with the pain he must have been going through. I felt sure this death, albeit not a good way to bring about change, would bring our family closer now. But it wasn't to be.

Siobhan felt on the outside of her father's family in death just as she had been in his life, the daughter not many seemed to know about at this funeral. She felt on the outside of her life looking in and, out of his three children, she received a few trinkets to remember him by. She hurt, not because of the money or material things, but because she had felt she was not recognised or respected.

I felt helpless over my estrangement from my son, but decided it was time to give up the struggle in my head and heart of wishing him home, and allow him to be free, to live his life through his choices. For a rescuer and a healer, that was extremely hard to accept. I loved him then, and I love him now, but I learned that love does not mean I own him. It means I love him enough to allow him to walk his soul path, to learn why he is here, what he came to experience and how amazing he is. Love exists everywhere, and Scott will feel that, sense that, know that, on some level; like all of us, his map will lead him to the right place for him, at the right and divine time, and maybe lead him home one day, He is, in my eyes, a brave soul journeying alone and I love him all the more for that.

We have arrived back to where this journey started, January 2009, and I am plastered. Thankfully, the programme of alcohol had not taken hold of me like my parents, but if you remember this is when my journey to write this book began. I should have stopped when I suffered the mini stroke and looked at my life at that point, but I carried on rescuing, healing, avoiding the signs, getting deeper in debt, more and more worried about life, unable to see a way ahead. One way or another God and that Holy part of you, your soul, will eventually stop you and you *will* see the signs on that soul map! Trust me!

Siobhan was now back home and we were living together, just as we had started out at the beginning of this decade. She had returned from Dubai in 2008 after deciding her relationship had come to a natural end. She left with only her clothes and her beloved dog, Nicco; nothing else mattered to her. I wished I had had the courage to do that many years before, perhaps then my vicious circles would have stopped much quicker.

When I broke my foot on the 13th January (remember, I fell over my vacuum cleaner. I knew one day cleaning would get me!), my worry over fending for myself expanded. With my leg in plaster, I could not earn at all but I had never asked anyone, ever, for help. I was Miss Stubborn, Miss Independent, but I certainly was not Miss World. I had piled on over two stones in weight and my confidence was at an all-time low. My life, like my body, was spiralling out of control.

As fate would have it, my sister was now living and working in Inveraray, Argyll – a most beautiful part of Scotland. And she gave me an offer I simply could not refuse. She had bought a beautiful old Rectory on the shores of Loch Fyne, and wondered if I would like to run a bed and breakfast for her. I would have a home for as long as I wanted, with no overheads, an income, and more importantly a new view on life. Without as much as a moment to think about it, BOOM, my soul replied with an astounding YES!

Within 6 weeks I was gone, leaving behind my daughter, my daughter-in-law, my granddaughter and her new baby sister, born 2 days before I moved. Debbie had met a wonderful man called John, and together they were all my family; even now, he is like a son to me, and always there if I need any help! It is so sad that Scott's other little daughter – born to his new partner – has not been part of my life. She is my granddaughter, too, and I pray that one day she will get to know her Nana and all her family, and fall in love with us, as we will with her.

Life in Inveraray taught me a lot. I painted and decorated a seven-bed guest house and ran it like clockwork. I created a new garden, and my sister and I used our creative flair to make it a home for tourists from all over the world who visited this old Royal town. I loved the challenges it gave me as the ratings went from zero to the top three in the area. I hosted, cooked, cleaned – of course – managed, and looked after people from all countries and walks of life every day. Sometimes my workload was over 60 hours a week.

By October 2010, I was still trying to pay off my debts. No matter what I paid to my credit cards, more was added on in interest than was actually paid off, which meant the debt just never went down. I was working all hours and, although grateful for a roof and a wage, I felt this vicious financial circle was never ending. I had gone here to change my life, but now my years of propping up a shop and giving to others were catching up on me, and that pressure was building yet again. On top of this, Dick wanted to buy my share of the villa, but I felt it was worth more than he wanted to pay me, so I refused to let it go. I needed that money for my future, for my debt, for my old age!

(Soul note: Listen to your words, NEED; you could hardly pay for this villa, pay your debt, pay for a holiday to the villa, but you were allowing this possession to hold you to your past, to rule your future! Why did you want to hold onto anything that connected you to pain. Let it go. Like your son, let it be free!)

One day, a knowing clarity came over me and I realised that none of this mattered. I was not going to be remembered in my life journey for the villa I once had, or for the men who had mistreated me, but for the strong divine woman I was. Amazing freedom came with the words 'LET IT GO'. I simply got up one morning and I understood clearly that the feeling of freedom, of self-worth, of loving myself, was far more important, more inspiring, more fulfilling than anything or anyone. It was more important than needing to prove my worth through the money in this villa share, so I agreed to sell my share for less than I had expected to get for it. I would then be truly free of my connection to my past, and that alone was worth its weight in gold. Freedom felt amazing!

The money paid off some debts and then, thanks to the help of an earth angel called Jeremy – a solicitor in England who had been advising me – I looked at ways of clearing what was left. I was sitting one day with a huge pile of papers and information about consolidating and clearing debt when, out of this massive pile of hundreds of sheets of information on my lap, one sheet fell to my feet. Oh, that soul was surely tuning in now, guiding me into a new understanding of my journey. After reading this piece of random information, I discovered that due to me not owning property or having anything of any value, I could declare myself bankrupt and my debt would be wiped clear. That was an immense insight.

It was only then I got it; I understood that when you have nothing, you have nothing to lose – and fear will never win again! You are simply free to be all you are and can be. Feeling that freedom from fear, even now, makes me smile! So 7 days after applying for bankruptcy in early December 2010, I lost 'everything', all I had ever worked for, even my beliefs about money and struggle, and my old beliefs about my credibility. But this was imperative for my new journey.

It was also to become the basis of every decision I would make, as now my soul was free, my heart was free, and my Ego mind that was the slave to my past thoughts, was free. Having nothing felt immense!

I began this new century tied to a man that I don't believe ever soulfully loved me, and in this very busy decade I had lost my beautiful soul mate, my Nany, my loving and handsome dad, my amazing son (in a different way), and my ex-husband. I had lost my business, lost my homes, lost my way! The signs were all there: LET IT GO!

Let go of the struggle, the battle, the dramas, the stories, the need to rescue and heal for fear of not being loved, the fear of not being good enough, of being rejected but yet had happened anyway. And I ended this decade in the best place I had been in all my life – and *with nothing*!

I had nothing, and yet I had it all. I had got it at last and my 'story' was no longer driving this vehicle on my journey; my soul was now firmly taking front seat. I had finally heard it speak, softly and lovingly from my heart, and trusted it completely.

Alchemy calls this stage Distillation, and it would seem I was catching up! It is the stage of creating something purer, where the soul drives the body and not the Ego. Finally I may be getting this alchemy!

Chapter 7

Decade: 2011 till now

2011 began my true soul recovery, my own deep healing, and an understanding of who I was on the planet. I was not my thoughts any more, or anyone else's thoughts about me for that matter; I was not just a mum, a nana, or a landlady of this beautiful bed and breakfast. I was now able to begin my amazing soul journey and mission properly, since that special soul reading now 10 years before.

Strange things were happening to me, and I was sensing, seeing, feeling, simply knowing more than ever before. I was waking up in the night speaking in a strange language, sometimes even singing in a strange language, which I now know to be the language of Light or Light Language. I could feel beings around me in the dead of night. I could not always see them, but I KNEW they were there! I had no fear now. With my mind in balance with my heart, I was completely at one with my life. I am telling **you** this, but for a long time I was sure that folk would think I had finally lost the plot.

*(Soul note: Don't backtrack now! Watch your language and how you speak of yourself, judgement of the self is soul-destroying. BELIEVE in you and your truth! Having these gifts does not make you strange; it makes you powerful, unique, and empowered. It makes you **YOU**, a beautiful soul with an immense heart and a powerful and balanced mind.)*

I knew instinctively the time was coming for this new work 'Science of the Heart' to enter my life. For the past 10 years it had remained in the forefront of my mind and my heart and I knew one day it would be shown to me in some form. I just did not know that this journey I had been on was part of it, and that my life was the template for this book so that many could understand it. Just as your journey is your soul's expansion programme, this was mine. We all have our genetic patterns, stories, habits and programmes. I had to reach a point where I had set my soul free, and for me, bankruptcy did that. It created a cleansing, a release from the old ways, patterns , programmes and habits for me, for my soul to really take control and take charge. With a clean slate and cleansed soul, I was now ready to accept this next part of my soul journey.

I had a feeling something was about to happen, and it did; I remember clearly an encounter of the GOD-ly kind! It was and still is very difficult to find the right words to describe the feelings I experienced; it was divine and personal, and I will never forget what happened. I do struggle to explain this, as words can never do it justice, and so I feel it is best not to. I prefer to explain this part to the students of my work on a personal level.

To say it was Divine is not enough, but I am guided to simply say that this was my soul gift, my own personal empowerment for my new work, being downloaded into me; it is beyond words. The experience was healing, magical and soul-empowering, and my soul and its body vibrated in tune with the voice of Heaven.

When I awoke the next morning, I knew it was not a dream. I could remember all the details, including the words that were spoken to me. I was so excited, and the feelings I experienced took me back to the night my cloaked friend had come to me all those years ago when I was 8. I knew, simply knew without any doubt, something unique had finally been offered to me!

I called my friend Kyle, because he understood experiences like this. He'd had his fair share in his younger years, and he understood me, too. I excitedly shared my experience with him. It felt good to talk openly about this, and by speaking about it, it felt more real and tangible. Sharing it with a like-minded soul friend made it all the more special; anyone else would probably have said, 'Junsie, you have finally lost the plot!' But not Kyle. He was just as excited as I was, and I want to say right now: thank you for that, my young soul friend, you helped this old woman remain sane and grounded!

Things seemed to begin happening more after this encounter. I was also learning about Divine timing, which was not my strong point, but I trusted everything would come to me when it was meant to which would be simply perfect for my soul to begin the work.

In November 2011, I travelled from Argyll to hold an empowering and large workshop on 11/11/11 which was simply amazing. The energy was sublime and all 36 souls who came enjoyed sharing this special planetary day as a group. During this year, my new work had begun, and the workshops, which were to be called Empowerments, had been downloaded. I held the very first two Empowerments of this new work, Science of the Heart, days after my 11/11/11 workshop.

It felt surreal to be finally offering my own work, and I will be forever grateful to the first eight souls who trusted me with their hearts. The work was beautiful, the Empowerments – which are encoded energy alignments – felt amazing, and I felt extremely humbled that I was finally doing this work. I was teaching my divine mission, to help souls empower themselves, to become the best version of themselves that they can be.

After all these exciting new experiences, I went back to Inveraray, but I missed my daughter and her little baby girl, Mya, and my other granddaughters so much. I carried on through Christmas and saw in another New Year. Another granddaughter from Siobhan, whom she called Ayla, was born in January 2012, and then my first grandson arrived a month later, on Valentine's Day. I began missing all these amazing children, my family, and extended spiritual family at home.

The year started off with these two births in two months, then in March Mum transitioned peacefully – she was eighty years old – ending yet another part of the soul story. Her journey was over and she was back home with her beloved Jackie.

More change was on the horizon as I had been noticing many more signs lately. It was so easy to feel them and see them now that my head was clear of confusion and fear. I felt a new chapter of life was about to begin and, after a quiet summer in the bed and breakfast, I knew it was time to go back home. So I left beautiful Inveraray, in August 2012, with great love in my heart for the family I had left behind there, the people, and the beauty of Argyll. I miss it, but I know it had served its healing purpose, and I trusted that wherever I was going would be perfect, too.

I was invited to attend Hay House's 'I Can do It' conference in Glasgow in September 2012 by my friend David, and it was while I was there that something changed for me. A revelation and an inspiration occurred. When I began writing my story in 2009, this book was not about Alchemy; it was simply 'my look at my life' and a deep need to put on paper all the dramas, stories, the ups and many downs that I had gone through. It had begun with my Ego telling me that folk would not believe this life I had led, it sounded like a Hollywood blockbuster. And, trust me, much of my journey even now has never been included in this book!

It had never occurred to me at that time that the importance of this story was not about my Ego's dramas, but instead it was about the journey from my head to my heart, a journey of words that would support my work Science of the Heart. So I set about changing the script and the way it was delivered so that students of the work – and hopefully you, dear soul friend – would understand the journey of the soul with all its genetics, its programmes and downloads from birth, its patterns, habits and addictions, its fears and its triumphs. I wanted to change it from a tale of woe to a tale of WOW!

I am an ordinary woman with an ordinary life, a nana to six amazing children, a mum to two amazing children, and I am no different to most of the seven billion souls who occupy our world. I am not a guru, a soul with extra special talents, or anything so unique that no-one else could do this. I was simply a Scottish 'soldier' from the Light Brigade, a light worker who was asked to deliver a script of sorts, with a powerfully loving message to relay to her world! And that message was and is, Science of the Heart. It has finally come, after all those years of waiting for it.

The work comes when I am ready in my soul to receive it. I had been given the information for the first two Empowerments, and I was informed that there was going to be a third Empowerment. I loved that I was also being taught patience and Divine timing with this work. The first two opened up the heart centre to allow more love, more heartfelt choices, and more decisions to flow, and it was beautiful to watch the changes it brought to those first eight souls. This work was offering tools and healing to enable them to find their own truth, their divinity, their unique hearts and who *they* were on the planet.

On going home to Lanarkshire, more of this work began to filter through, and eventually a third Empowerment was born. This level was beautiful, and it helped souls discover their true authentic self through their now open heart. It brought in their soul map, and by going on a journey back in time to address all the twists and turns, highs and lows, seeing the journey for what it truly was, it helped heal any darkness and allowed that soul a deeper understanding of their journey without labels, without Ego, and without drama. It brought about a peace within, an acceptance of the journey without judgement.

The lead weights, the heavy baggage I used to cart about every day, had gone. Even my body was two stone lighter. And the only booming I heard now was my beating heart and the sound of all that heavy baggage that had been carried around for sixty years finally dropping.

(Note to my patient Soul: In all those years of reaching out through psychic readings for the answers through others who never even knew me, I should have simply reached out to you, for you knew exactly what I needed and who I was. You could read me like this book, you understood me, and yet I forgot about you. But maybe that was the perfect plan anyway, for I may never have been guided to write this book or ask for that soul reading which changed my life. Everything is ALWAYS perfect!)

It is never too late to turn your journey around, to take the time to listen to your own heart, your own soul, and know who you are, no matter where you are in your life right now. Go and find a sheet of paper and draw out your soul map from birth till this point in time; look at your whole journey, look at all your twists and turns, the points on that road that were wonderful or hard, and discover where your Ego mind was in charge, or where your heart was in charge. I guarantee your heart and soul will always have made the right choices, and those choices will always have been perfect, fast, flowing, inspirational, and transforming. If that part of the map fell immediately into place without struggle, that is your heart and soul offering you advice. If your Ego was driving... well, look at me, I spent most of my life like a rubber band, pinging from lost cause to lost soul!

I was guided to create beautiful high vibrational aura sprays to assist and support the process of transformation or Alchemy. They assist, heal, balance, and restore the vehicle that is your body, and the extended bodies in the auric field. I trusted that my soul would simply know how to create them as I had never worked with oils or anything like that before. I simply trust, and follow my heart, and my soul does all the work. They are high vibrational, energetic, empowered aura sprays that assist the journey, and if anyone had told me 10 years ago this would actually happen and I would be able to work this way, I would never have believed them.

Somehow my soul got it, and held onto that inner truth, and when the time was perfect it all came together like the jigsaw puzzle I mentioned earlier in the book. So please, don't fear if you feel your life is a mess, that there is no time to make changes, that it has all slipped by and you simply took a wrong road, a long detour, or got on the wrong Alchemy train. Let your soul guide you, allow your powerful mind to come into balance with your loving, trusting heart, and your journey will take on a new glow – a golden one.

As I develop and raise my own vibration, I have been given more of this amazing work. Empowerment four is life-changing; it is all about recognising our soul patterns, the programmes we run that may not be ours but given to us by our parents, and genetic downloads.

It is about our habits, our addictions and limiting beliefs, about who we are as a soul with a body. It is deep, it is extremely powerful, and it does what it says, it restores the soul, connects the heart, and balances the mind. And it is crucial for personal Alchemy.

In 2014, I was also guided to create the final three Empowerments creating a total of seven. This final stage is about your own temple, your body. Previous empowerments looked at the heart and all its emotions, the mind and the patterns, programmes and limiting beliefs it can hold. Finally, we look at the effects of all of this on the major organs of the body, together with the head area with emphasis on the higher chakras and intuitive centres, and the auric field and extended layers of who we are.

SEVEN empowerments making for the SEVEN stages of Alchemy, and all given when the time is perfect.

Soul summary~ July 2014

As I finish the last few pages of this long running script, I sit with both my feet up, resting them from a fall. And I have to laugh, because it was a fall 5 years ago that caused me to break my foot, which in turn created the time and impetus for me to begin this story.

So here we are again, full circle. I not only hurt one, but both feet this time, making doubly sure I was and am immobile long enough to sit down and finish what I'd started. I have been editing this work for months now, and I feel I am simply being told that time is up, the journey is complete, so STOP and get this book finished and out to the souls who are ready to begin their own alchemical journey.

Someone recently asked me if I have regrets.

Many times in the past I would have said yes, or 'if only'!

If only my mother had never left me as a baby, creating issues for me with rejection, fear, separation, and many patterns that followed. If only she had not placed so many of her issues on my little shoulders. If only my parents had never argued, if only they had been more alike. If only I had followed my own passion for teaching and not become what my parents wanted me for me; they never respected my own choices. If only I had not married Tom so young, or rushed to leave home and away from my parents' issues. If only I had never taken him back when I knew in my heart that he did not respect me. If only I had never fallen for a man who, unknown to me at that time, mirrored so much of me with his rescuing, his face for the world, his need to look good, powerful and successful to everyone but who also had a lack of respect for me. If only

I had been stronger with my son and pleaded with him to stay in my life. If only I could have saved my parents from destroying their lives with alcohol. If only I had respected money more. If only I had respected myself more!

If only does not exist in my world any more, and RESPECT where respect is due!

I respect and love my soul, myself; my body, mind and heart – the only respect that is required. I respect all my decisions, even when I look back over my soul map and realise just how many weird and wonderful ones I made at different times. But had I not made them, I would never have written this soul story and understood the journey. I respect my parents and all the generations of my soul family for everything they taught me, gave me, and allowed me to experience in many varied ways. And finally, because of all my experiences, I realised my passion to teach.

I respect both my partners for their part in my soul journey, as they were truly my mirrors and my teachers. They loved me in their chosen way, for I, too, was part of their soul journey, their teacher and, on a soul level, I will always love them for that. I respect my son's choices to explore his world his way, without his family around him; what a brave man he has turned out to be. I respect the soul decisions of my amazing daughter, who has repeated many of my own patterns, showing me that genetic patterning and childhood programming truly affects us all. She is an inspiration, not only in her world, but to her daughters, too, and those girls have chosen an amazing woman for their mother. I respect my extended family and how they have never become the victims of their soul journeys.

So in looking back on my soul map of this life journey, do I have any regrets? NO. It was all perfect – the hard times, the good times, the fun times, and the tough times, because without all of those parts of this journey I would not be who I am today. I am peaceful and happy inside, I have fallen in love with life and with whom I am on the planet, inside and out. I am grateful for everything I have experienced, everyone who has ever loved me, and I them. I'm even grateful for losing everything including my pride in bankruptcy, for in that moment of being stripped bare, the freedom from fear was magnificent. I knew I was everything I would ever need now, in that present moment (for it was a gift to my soul) and in the future. I understood that I already had everything, love from inside of me being the biggest realisation. With fear gone, love for my own soul simply filled the void, and the balance of life was simply restored. Anything I wished to be, become, and offer in service to my world was now inside my heart and soul; there is now no need to search outside of me for the answers.

I was and I AM truly empowered. What an amazing soul gift this journey is and has been, and when I look back on mine, through the eyes of my soul, I speak from my heart when I tell you:

- * have no regrets

- * forgive the past, let it go

- * live in the now, the gift of the present

- * remove fear from your Ego/mind, bring it into balance with your immense heart

- * and see the golden opportunities in all your experiences.

That way you will not become the victim of limited beliefs, patterns, programmes and habits that may never have been yours anyway! And please remember, Alchemist, that you have a seventh sense – the sense of humour, one of brightness, happy memories and positivity that truly helps to lighten those dark patches on that map, to enable you see the nuggets of gold within. Let it shine like an inner beacon of love from your heart, helping you see the road ahead clearly and with gratitude for every part you have travelled to so far.

So, my friend, enjoy your soul journey. Hop aboard the Alchemy train and remember, that heavy baggage you begin your journey with will become lighter and brighter at every stop. Be kind to you, love all parts of you, heart, mind, body and soul. Appreciate your uniqueness and look at your journey now through the eyes of your soul.

I wish you love for your heart, wisdom for your mind, health for your body, and joy, peace and abundance for your soul's journey! Your alchemical transformation will create great change, not only for you but for your children and their generations to come, and of course, for your world; our world.

Alchemy

Some will explain Alchemy as a science of chemical processes, of turning base metals into precious metals, lead into gold, a science which uses external forms of matter that already exist and mix them up to create something new. Others will explain alchemy as a spiritual science, a science of the soul that comes from inner understanding, inner wisdom that creates great growth and personal transformation. My journey has been one of spiritual Alchemy.

The reason I chose to open my story up this way – and I promise you, many of my dramas, reactionary mind decisions, and resulting doom, gloom (and boom) were omitted due to repetition – was to endeavour to simply walk my talk, to explain my work by my own example. I wanted to look back at my own life and see how the experiences of my individual mind had stopped my personal Alchemy from realising the gold of the Universal mind.

For so many years I constantly looked outside of myself for happiness, for respect, for change, and most importantly for the truth. All along those 7 decades of my life, that truth was right there, inside my heart. Learning to love myself, warts and all, was my biggest gift; it brought a golden glow of peace within my soul that I appreciate daily.

I may not be the richest person in this world materially, but I now understand that richness comes in many forms. It mirrors itself in self-love and love of others, kindness, gratitude, sharing, and caring. It shows itself as many things to many people, which could range from self-belief to self-respect... for alchemy is not about what lies outside of you, but is about what lies inside of you. It is the gift of self-discovery, transformation and acceptance. It is the gift of inner peace and balance.

Science of the Heart teaches this. That it is the soul's rite of passage into personal evolution and evolvement to live from the wisdom of the heart and not the limitations of the Ego mind.

Going back through my soul map from birth, exploring each decade of my life, I can see clearly all the generational patterns and programmes that impacted upon me. As a child I had downloaded many parental issues, patterns and behaviours, and their programmes morphed into mine. I even took on board some of those outside of my family and made them my own; I truly was a generous soul at heart. It is no wonder that I felt I rode an eternal hamster wheel, struggling to keep going at times, exhausted by the repeating steps I was oblivious to. Looking back in this way was the most healing gift I have ever given myself.

I recognised that my life had spanned 7 decades and, for the purposes of explaining my own personal journey, I can also refer to those decades through the 7 stages of

Alchemy. Please, dear soul traveller, do not lose heart. You certainly do not need to be my age to 'get it'. You are unique, so your alchemical transformation can happen today, tomorrow, or indeed in 7 years; that will simply be your choice. It is said that life runs in seven year cycles, so maybe this could be your key to your soul map. However you do it, know that there is no wrong or right way. I simply urge you to look back, to not only face and forgive the pain, fears or loss, but at the gifts, the unexplored nuggets, the wisdom you hold to turn your personal dull lead into brilliant gold!

We have spoken of the generational programmes of behaviour we take on board, the patterns we pick up, the habits, addictions, and beliefs we adopt from external sources that can shape our journey, and I hope you can see these from my own life. However, scientists are now researching other factors that may affect our human soul, called Generational Epigenetics; recent research shows that not all that affects our lives lies within our DNA, and that the effects of certain circumstances, environment, trauma, diet, emotional behaviour, and even phobias from our forefathers and mothers can become inherited.

Much work is being done in this field to have a greater understanding of how these inherited memories may be passed on. Like genetic memory, it could mean that we may even switch on some of the memories, like traumas which have happened during the lives of our ancestors, and how these events may have had an impact upon the eggs or sperm inside a growing foetus within the womb of its mother. This can have an effect on up to three generations. The egg that will become you is created in the foetus of your mother while she was a foetus within your grandmother's womb, so you could liken yourself to a Russian doll.

As I have said before, I am no scientist and so I ask you to research this if it feels right for you. There are many wonderful scientists helping to bridge the gap between science and spirituality, or science of the soul.

I wanted this book to flow, like any life journey should, and lots of 'stuff' was omitted because I seemed to simply remain in stuck patterns for much of my adult life. The book was written not for the purpose of sensational dramas, nor did I want anyone to think I was a victim or trying to manipulate the 'poor me' energy. I wanted to simply talk my walk, and in doing so help those who trust my work, Science of the Heart. The book and its soul map are simply a guide for you to recognise your own 'stuff'.

I was also guided to offer an insight into the stages of alchemical change we encounter as souls on this human journey. To allow my map to flow better, I was guided to put this section at the end; that way you can choose to either refer to it as you read each chapter, or wait until you have finished.

Originally my Ego began this book, it was the 'no-one would believe it' attitude to life. Call it victimhood or drama queen, I don't even recognise that part of me now, but as the story began its journey and I started to explore my own soul, I began to see the nuggets within. I saw the Alchemy that my ancient wise soul already understood, as I got out of my head and into my heart. I truly hope it instils the same exploration in you!

Alchemy Stage 1 – Calcination
(Relate to 1950s)

Calcination represents the process of fire, a burning within the self of the energies we can repress due to trauma, even the projection of others' thoughts, their egos, feelings and emotions which affect us deeply. So for me, it was the trauma of being rejected and abandoned by my mum at 8 months old, and the long-lasting effects this had on my young body and soul that began my patterns.

I had witnessed many mind games which my parents played out in their stories, then *their* stories were projected onto me as a child. The result was patterns and fears which I was unaware of most of my life. As a soul of this tender age, I did not have the ability to understand all of the issues adults had created around me at that time, or even make a conscious choice not to take them on board. It may be later on in your journey, soul friend, that we realise how others may have affected our lives, good and bad, how *their* egos and behaviour may have created a mirror of this within ourselves. So this process of Calcination allows us to begin the change, burn away negative patterning, take control once again of who we are, be in touch with our true essence, that soul part that is not limited by our minds or bodies.

When this process occurs, it allows each soul to bring negative, painful, limiting issues, and feelings to the surface, to experience them fully, thank them for all the positive effects they also had, and then surrender them into the fire to burn away, offering you freedom from the hurt, traumas, thoughts, and pain, and allowing you to experience your true soul, your beautiful golden essence.

Looking back over my own soul map, I recognised my childhood traumas and fears and, through this process of Calcination, allowed the purifying fire of this stage to offer freedom from those thoughts, those traumas or fears. This is the beginning of change for you, recognition of deep-rooted patterns and memories, understanding how they became yours, forgiving them, and releasing them through fire or even inner fiery passion for transformation.

It can help you to release and clear old thought forms of anger, regret, frustration, even patterns that limit who you are, inherited habits or addictions, painful memories, by committing them to paper; don't read them back, just know you have done this. Then place the paper safely in a fireproof bowl – preferably out in your garden – and set it alight, asking your soul, higher guidance, to remove the negative effects from your cells.

At the end of my first decade on the planet I was seven-and-a-half years old, and I was not aware of any of this at that time. But when my inner process of change began, I did go through this time of my life and wrote about all my heartfelt issues, my 'stuff', and you can see how I explored my past from this book... Yes, I did set it alight and it certainly helped me release much; it was a beginning, a feeling of taking some of my power back during years of feeling lost and loss.

Love is the FIRE of Life; it either consumes or purifies

Heart affirmation: I sit by the fireside of my heart and ignite the passion of my soul into great visions of golden peace, forgiveness, gratitude, balance, and freedom within me.

Alchemical Stage 2 – Dissolution
(Relates to 1960s)

As this, my second decade on earth, was coming to a close, I looked at the second stage of Alchemy which is called Dissolution.

Dissolution, the second process in our alchemical transformation, has the addition of the element water. From the ashes of the fires of Calcination – the first stage of Alchemy – we can then look at the emotions of our lives at this time. What did the soul feel during this time when those repressed feelings were taking hold and needed to be washed away?

The feelings which we attach to opinions, thoughts, actions, and reactions, the beliefs that we begin to form and the resulting attitudes that were being created; we really should look into them to see, feel, know if they are simply repressed feelings or facts. This stage of change can feel difficult as we penetrate the illusions we hold, examining anxiety, fear, denial of much around us. However, when you are able to work through this stage, and pour the 'water of life' onto the issues or illusions we experience – be that through the release of tears through sadness and joy – we create an alchemical change of state.

We let go, we dissolve the hard facts or illusions our minds create, and we find, through the use of our emotions, a 'solution'.

(The water element is related to our emotions and feminine nurturing side.)

I can see how in my own life and soul path this decade created not just a problem with my thinking, but my thoughts also had an effect on my emotions. Life was mirroring back to me through the actions, thoughts, and emotions of my loved ones what my soul was experiencing on the journey. We are taught and expected to trust our family, even if some of their ways may seem wrong to us, or not feel right for us. If we are not fully in our own power at a tender age, having to rely on others to survive, we blindly trust this part of our journey because we cannot see the end result of other's actions on our lives.

Dissolution is all about following our bliss, being in the flow, using the conscious part of our mind to let go of control, and allowing anything that is buried within us to rise, opening those floodgates to release and allow new energy to flow in. When the combination of the conscious mind and subconscious mind integrate as one, this flow of energy is blissful, because the illusions then dissolve and our truth is left for us to see and feel.

Normally, as an alchemical stage in soul evolution, dissolution takes part in the genital area of the body, and I feel this makes sense. Our own inner passions begin to fire up through stage one, which is Calcination, through our experiences of life as a child, and then as our bodies transform from that child into an adolescent, many inner changes happen due to hormones and our new-found emotions which begin to appear. We may now become more in touch with who we are on this journey. Calcination worked on our minds, our Ego, destroying the deceptions of our thoughts through burning them off by fire. Dissolution works on our hearts to assist us in releasing buried emotions that stop us transforming into our own true soul selves. I can really understand this part of the process in the journey, as I truly did not wish to take on the emotions, thoughts, and feelings of my parents.

In the smoking mirrors of life, my parents were really teaching me how NOT to be, and were truly magnificent teachers for my soul, as I knew in my heart that I would never raise a soul in this way. I was shown by deconstruction how not to be! I am sure many can relate to this; the ways of our parents' lives can either make us victims of our own journey, or embrace the alchemical changes for our own soul journey. The choice is most definitely yours to take, and I am so happy I chose the later because I am now, free of my parents' choices.

This stage of change, is all about setting old emotions free, allowing the soul to look into the murky waters of life (made from the ashes of calcinations and waters of dissolution), then to allow the silt and mud to settle in the water, and clarity will return. Enjoy the process, for it will heal your soul!

Affirmation: I lie in the warm, clear waters of the soul's womb and allow this life giving element to heal me. I love my soul with all my heart. I honour the wombs of all my grandmothers who have held that sacred space within me, and I them.

Alchemical Stage 3 - Separation
(Relates to 1970s)

Now this third stage of Alchemy is called Separation Never a truer statement for this time in my journey. In this part of my soul map, I had separated from my family, my sister, my friends, and my special soul mate – my Nany – to embark on a 'new' journey with my husband.

In this alchemical process the individual or soul should see themselves in two parts – the life we create, which is impacted from where we came, and our world of reality which **SHOULD** be different to the one we create. Can you see my dilemma? I separated from one reality and created another reality that really was, in essence, the same as before!

What was my soul doing?

When our soul represses deep thoughts and emotions, it creates another smoking mirror, one where our reality becomes twisted like the strange mirrors at the funfair. You know it is you, but it looks – and yes, feels like – someone completely different. This process of separation should enable you to see your Ego for what it is, as you should have been able to separate YOU from your Ego self. Ego is that inner voice that keeps you small, that tells your inane thoughts how powerful and right THEY are.

This part of you, which you may have hopefully burned off in the fires of Calcination (your mind – stage 1 of Alchemy), then the many resulting feelings from that stage which should have been, or maybe were released and washed away in Dissolution (your heart – stage 2 of Alchemy), so that by now, only those parts of you that you truly wish to keep are left! No more Ego should live on in this part of the soul journey, or does it?

Oh dear, something went wrong in my personal Alchemy here, and this stage was definitely missed. Hopefully, my soul would make sure I got this later on, in my own perfect and divine time. Our souls are so ancient, so wise, so unconditional, and we most definitely understand this soul direction and connection with its loving wisdom and peaceful and balanced state when we are in tune with our true soul energy. However, when the Ego gets a hold of us through our thoughts, our mind, it makes life hard and can stop life happening. And it did for me.

Please remember, Ego does not mean being 'big-headed'. Many have translated it to mean this; you know how some will say, 'what an ego she or he has!' I certainly was not big-headed, I was small-voiced, had small ambitions, small dreams, in fact, small everything. Ego simply means 'edging GOD out', not listening to your true authentic soul self, your heart, your eternal wise soul, choosing instead to listen to your thoughts, created by your mind.

Your mind is an immense tool. Used correctly, it always tries to help you, to protect you, to keep you safe the best way it can. It can be ever so powerful, and yet when it is SEPARATED from the heart and the soul, it can be a dangerous tool. When our mind is working in harmony, in balance with our heart and soul as an authentic spiritual team, we become a unified soul with all parts of this vehicle working together for the highest and greatest good. This is when Alchemy happens, and your journey becomes easier, when the journey from the head to the heart unifies all parts of who you are, making your soul strong, creating a soul-full life.

Affirmation: As I look into the mirror of my soul, I separate the small voice within that keeps me in fear, trapped in a dark world of impossibilities to hear the thoughts of my extensive beautiful heart who says loudly: you are immense, you are powerful, you are LOVE. Shine your loving, powerful, bright soul light into the world of ALL possibilities, for all to see. In doing so, you allow others to shine and reflect this light back to you and the world.

Alchemical Stage 4 - Conjunction
(Relates to 1980s)

Now I can see, although completely unknown to me this time of my journey, that my Ego was the only driver, my heart was just its passenger. SOS! Sheep Only Syndrome.

In this stage of Alchemy. we should be beginning to know the real 'us', what this journey is really all about, recognising that we are creative, loving, grounded souls, and in many ways during this decade of my own journey, I caught glimpses of this. Now a new decade was beginning and I had begun a new part of my journey, but I can also see that by the end of this decade I was NOT centred, life was not balanced. Instead, I was giving every part of me out to those around me and not looking, or feeling, or understanding what was happening to me inwardly!

I can look back from 1980 with compassion, with love, and see who I was at this point, and who I had become as another decade began. Some parts of me had gone, dissolved through the process of fire and water, and now new parts of me were beginning to emerge from the smoke of the fire, like the phoenix rising from the ashes, with passion and desire for more.

But what I failed to see was that 'my desires and passions' were fuelled by another, they were not my own heartfelt passions, they were the dreams of others. Would anything stir my heart into discovering who I truly was? Maybe the next decade would provide the impetus and stimulus to truly begin my own soul journey; I was running a little late, my Alchemy train was behind schedule. This fourth stage states that you cannot give more to another than you give to yourself, and this was exactly what I was doing, now more than ever!!

Affirmation: I love myself, my body, my mind, my heart, my emotions, my beliefs, my creations, my words, my sound, my life, my journey, my dreams and goals unconditionally, daily. I, as my true and beautiful Soul, with my loving heart and creative, balanced mind, and my beautiful body as my vehicle, am the most important part of my journey, all as one, as above so below. I am sole/soul-ly responsible for everything and for every part of my soul journey, and I bask in this knowing.

Alchemical Stage 5 - Fermentation
(Relates to 1990s)

This fifth decade of my journey relates to the stage of Alchemy which is called Fermentation, but when I look at this powerful yet traumatic time in my story, I can see all the other stages of Alchemy, too – Calcination, Dissolution, Separation and Conjunction all wrapped up in this one decade!

Was my alchemical process finally catching up with me? Was I finally, at long last, removing the fancy designer wrapper off my life story and seeing what the journey was really about? And what had opened my soul's eyes? Sometimes it is in the darkness that we see the light.

What did this mean for me looking at my personal transformation during this time? In Alchemy it states that Fermentation is about the decomposition of the dead self, that on a deep level you begin to realise your own deficiencies, see your own faults and, by looking into your own dark shadows and going through the dark night of the soul, all that is no longer required can be illuminated. You can begin to see what you finally have to change and release from your life.

When our darkness or our shadow self is embraced, it can be healed, and this soul part of you urges you to step further and deeper into the now finely-tuned fire of Calcination again, refining you more and more, stripping away all the dead parts of you that no longer serve your soul. Then, as a soul, you can fully understand your old ways, patterns, and programmes, heal them, forgive them, and then move on into a new way of being and living.

Like the elusive phoenix, this is the point when I personally should have taken no more. I should have risen from this last decade with immense self-worth, self-belief, and self-understanding of my place on this planet, how brave I was to experience all this darkness, and to fully embrace feeling brand new and beautiful.

However, my Alchemy train was always running late, and I still had some processing to do. I was certainly getting to this stage, because my soul was now becoming more involved in my journey and helping lead me to new levels of being, of learning, and possibly remembering on a soul level who I truly was. But as I learned to let go of the old patterns that the Ego mind was still tuned into – the 'story or the drama' – my soul was now desperately shouting, 'Get out of your head, get out of your own way, leave the "story" behind, reach higher!'

I may be a slow burner and a slow learner, but on some level I know I was getting this message loud and clear!

Affirmation: I listen to the sacred and unique sound of my soul's calling, reaching out to me from within, holding me in immense love, gratitude, and inner peace. My soul is who I am, and my 'I AM' is truly my soul. I let go of all that does not sing in harmony with my soul. The lyrics of my soul song are truly beautiful when all notes are completely in tune; my soul sound is unique.

Alchemical Stage 6 - Distillation

(Relates to 2000s)

This stage of Alchemy is called Distillation, and it is the process we go through whereby another wash, another cycle in that washing machine of life, happens; where parts of the Ego or personality that no longer work with who you are becoming, are finally washed away.

Sometimes, we humans think that our success is measured by what we have materially gained in our lifetime, what label we give others, by the job we do, and that the opinions of us are dependent on how they see that success in us. So we often become attached to material things and the need to be 'successful' at any cost. This stage of Alchemy calls for us to release that attachment to everything, and feel this detachment as a form of love for the self, the soul. Having bankrupted myself, I released myself from everything and everyone, so I REALLY understood this! That feeling of freedom is truly immense. It was the best gift I had ever been given and it came from my own soul (and my creator, God).

This form of love comes from a higher aspect and is usually felt once we let go of our attachments to the end result or the future. This is how I teach: be open to the flow of life, even in a simple meditation, don't attach any outcome on the process. Let life and energy flow. Always aim for the highest good and the best possible outcome for your soul!

Distillation helps wash away the darkness of the self, revealing our deeper intuitive self or soul in a purer form, one of lightness and oneness. Finally, after all these years of clouded self-judgement, I was clearly becoming at one with my soul.

I am not suggesting everyone reading this should go bankrupt; that was simply part of *my* process, *my* journey, but if you are holding onto situations or people through fear, through *need* of any sort, let go and see what happens.

Affirmation: I allow my soul to enjoy freedom in all ways, I trust my heart to love me, my mind to empower me, and my soul to drive my vehicle, which is my beautiful body. I go with the flow of life peacefully, joyfully, abundantly, and completely in love with myself in the mystery tour which is my life's journey.

Alchemical Stage 7 - Coagulation

(Relates to 2011 til now)

This last stage in Alchemy is called Coagulation; the balance of opposites creates a balance, or harmony within, so you can move easily between the realms of earth and Heaven, matter and spirit.

When a soul has accomplished this stage of unification of all within, male/female, heart/mind, they are able to join soul and body on all levels. This enables them to separate themselves from everything that could hinder their ascension, their enlightenment with the divine. This IS the phoenix finally rising from the ashes from that first stage of the fires of Calcination!

Balance is imperative now. Balance of heart and mind, male and female within, body and soul, matter and spirit. And although I had a greater understanding now of my heart, it was imperative that my mind was also included in the whole picture. It was not my enemy. The tool I used for this was Neuro-Linguistic Programming (or NLP as it is called). Understanding the workings of my mind in this way helped me understand that I had assumed everyone thought like me. It helped me understand that other souls' mind maps could be very different; they could interpret their world and their thoughts in a different way. They may even word things differently. It taught me to never assume I should know how someone else thought, and that helped me understand not only my son's way of dealing with his life, but my ex–partners' ways, too.

A compassionate understanding of their own mind maps descended upon me, like the snow in the snow globe I was shown as a metaphor, a tool for confusion.

That globe reminded me how far I had come, as my head was clear, there was no snowstorm going on in there now, it had all settled and finally life felt crisp, clean, fresh and sparkling, with a quiet peaceful inner knowing that the storm was over and life was indeed eternal. My journey continues to refine itself and I see more gold as I pan through life, the silt falls away more easily now, washed away by my strong heart and empowered soul. I am becoming the best version of me, and in doing so, it reflects on those around me . Life is good. Life is golden!

I leave you with my last **Affirmation:** Like the phoenix, I rise from the ashes of my old life and settle joyfully into a new soul journey, one which is free from all restrictions, age, limitations, balanced in all ways, one which feels sacred, protected, and one which expands my cosmic heart into new but eternal ways. I fully integrate with my soul in the exciting mystery that is my journey as a soul with this beautiful body!

Acknowledgements

I wish to offer my heartfelt gratitude and deep love to my 'Earth' family who have all played their roles magnificently! My children, who have given me unconditional love, great lessons, growth, and amazing insight... Scott and Siobhan, love you both. You are truly beautiful, loving, wise, and immense souls.

I thank God daily for all my grandchildren (not forgetting my niece, Amy), who all give great cuddles, allow me to be a child again, and remind me to see joy in the simplest of ways!

To all who have helped my soul grow: my daughter-in law, Debbie, your beautiful young wisdom taught me never to judge other's choices; my sister, Cathie, who has always been there for me in so many ways, loving and supporting my sometimes crazy life; and her husband, David, who – with her – gave me an opportunity to heal my life and find myself in beautiful Inveraray.

And to my elders, who offered a grounded and 'interesting' foundation for this journey, especially my Nany Kate, who was my soul mate, surrogate mum, friend and mentor. To all of my ever-growing and extended family of like-minded friends, especially Dr David Hamilton, Debbie Clayton, Kyle Gray, and my soul friends, Gordon and Ben. Thank you all for your love and encouragement to write this book. I am grateful to Christine Mcpherson for her skilful editing, to Marion Menzies for casting a legal eye over the manuscript, and to Kim and Sinclair Macleod, of Indie Authors, World, who have encouraged, mentored, and assisted every step of the way in getting this book out there.

There are too many beautiful souls to mention by name, but special mention to all the souls who have embarked on their own alchemical journey through Science of the Heart, I am so grateful for your love and trust in this process; special thanks to Angie, Irene, Teresa, Lorna, Michelle, Alison, Sheila, and Julie, who trusted me with their hearts and souls on the very first Empowerment journey with this work!

Gratitude to two of the greatest teachers in my life – 'Tom' and 'Dick' (I changed their names in deep respect), as you truly helped my soul grow in so many ways. I am now ready to meet 'Harry', who may come along when Divine timing allows, and walk with me into a more peaceful, loving, balanced, soul-centred destination, having learned from both of your intense lessons and love. My heart will always find love for you both and thank goodness for that seventh sense, as I can look back now and find the joy, feel the good times we shared, and see the lessons as positive ones, without any pain or regret. I will truly always love you for sharing part of my life. Only ever love.

I just want to thank my soul for pushing 'me' to the limit, and my heart for listening!

Enjoy your own soul journey on the Alchemy train! Looking back at my mine, through the windows of my soul, I can now only see the immense scenery, the beautiful growth, and the amazing passengers, with the added excitement that the final destination is still to be revealed! ALL aboard!! And, dear Alchemist, remember to pack your seventh sense. It's so important, one we sometimes forget about – our sense of humour – it helps to lighten up the load and the road.

Finally, I'd like to share with you with a beautiful Lakota prayer which says so simply the essence of this story.

> *Teach me how to trust my heart, my mind, my intuition,*
> *My inner knowing, the senses of my body, the blessings of my spirit.*
> *Teach me to trust these things so that I may enter my sacred space*
> *And love beyond my fear*
> *And thus, walk in balance with the passing of each glorious sun.*

Great gratitude to you, dear fellow soul traveller. Thank you for taking time to read my soul story and if it creates even one light bulb moment, one act of forgiveness, one feeling of gratitude, happiness, or brings back great memories of your journey or even realisation of how you can heal the past truly live in balance, then it has done its work. It pleases my soul to know that although we are all unique and all our journeys different, the basis is self-love, and love for all, self-empowerment and empowerment of others, and self-respect and respect for all who have been part of our story.

May you live each day with love in your heart as you listen to the voice of your soul.

About The Author

June Moore has had many 'job titles', however, her passion now is helping others realise their 'soul full' potential . A Reiki Master, she has taught energy work, meditation, intuitive development, and unique workshops, and now, having worked on her own soul journey, she wishes to dedicate her path ahead to help others empower their unique soul map.

Her new work, Science of the Heart, is a journey through 7 Empowerments or energy alignments, a journey of spiritual alchemy for the ordinary soul. If you would like to know more about her new work, or understand more about your own soul journey , then check out her new web site.

www.scienceoftheheart.co.uk

Lightning Source UK Ltd.
Milton Keynes UK
UKOW05f0932050215

245701UK00007B/49/P